THE BRAIN FOLLOWS

WHY MENTAL HEALTH BEGINS WITH THE BODY

DR. JIM COSTELLO

The Brain Follows: Why Mental Health Begins With the Body

For permission requests, contact:

support@drjimcostello.com

Published by C7, Inc.

ISBN: 979-8-218-69055-7

First Edition

Disclaimer: The stories shared in this book are based on real experiences. Some names and identifying details have been changed to protect privacy. The information in this book is intended for educational and informational purposes only and is not a substitute for medical advice, diagnosis, or treatment, professional medical or psychological care. Always consult with a qualified healthcare provider before beginning any new exercise, wellness, or therapeutic program—especially if you have a history of medical or mental health conditions. The author and publisher disclaim any liability for injury or loss incurred as a result of the information presented herein.

DEDICATION

To my clients—

You came in carrying more than most people ever see. You walked in through overwhelm, burnout, shutdown, and chaos—and still, you stayed in the work. Some of you came searching for answers for yourselves. Others came carrying the weight of someone you love.

To the parents who brought their children—thank you. Thank you for your trust, your hope, and your willingness to believe that something different was possible. Your care helped shape the heart of this work.

You didn't always have the words for what you were feeling. But you stayed open. You kept showing up. And you reminded me—again and again—that real change doesn't start with mindset. It starts with the body.

To the practitioners—

Thank you for trusting me with the people you care for. Long before this process had a name or a structure, you saw its value. Your referrals weren't just professional—they were personal. You believed in this work before there was language for it, and that belief helped carry it forward.

To my family—

You've taught me more than any training ever could. The most important lessons I've learned about regulation, disconnection, and repair didn't come from theory—they came from living them with you. You reminded me that healing doesn't just happen in sessions or books. It happens in real life—in the mess and beauty of everyday relationships.

This book carries all of that. It carries you. And I'm deeply grateful.

—Jim

CONTENTS

PART IV
WHY LABELS ALONE DON'T LEAD TO LASTING CHANGE

ABOUT THIS BOOK

We've been told that healing happens in the mind: that with enough insight, intention, or effort, we can overcome anxiety, trauma, and emotional overwhelm. But what if we're not stuck from lack of effort, but because we've been starting in the wrong place?

In *The Brain Follows*, Dr. Jim Costello offers a powerful reframe: mental health doesn't begin with the brain. It begins with the body. Drawing on decades of clinical experience, personal story, and the latest in neurodevelopmental science, Costello introduces the Costello Method, a body-first framework for rewiring the stress response through movement, rhythm, and sensory integration.

This book is a roadmap for those who've tried everything. It's for the ones who have insight but no access. For those who know what to do, but still feel dysregulated.

Through clear explanations and human stories, *The Brain Follows* shows you how to:

- Understand the nervous system as the root of mental and emotional patterns.
- Reframe anxiety, ADHD, trauma, and shutdown as survival adaptations.

- Shift out of chronic stress, not through mindset, but through movement.
- Restore safety to the body, so the brain can finally let go.

It's a guide to remembering what your body has always known: When the body leads, the brain follows.

PREFACE

The Hurricane Named Adam

The first time I met Adam, it was like stepping into a storm.

He was in constant motion—bouncing, spinning, flapping his hands so fast they blurred. His feet barely touched the ground before he was off again, a whirlwind of nervous energy. His breath was shallow and rapid. His eyes never settled on one thing for long.

His parents looked like they hadn't slept in years.

They spoke to him gently, tried to guide him, but it was clear—Adam wasn't with them. His body was locked in fight-or-flight, running purely on instinct, his world a blur of sensation he couldn't organize.

This wasn't just hyperactivity.

This was deep dysregulation—his nervous system stuck in overdrive, unable to find its way back to calm.

And then I remembered something.

Stoney: The Horse Who Taught Me Everything

Years earlier, I had worked with a horse named Stoney—an old soul, worn from years of labor, his back stiff, his movements hesitant. I'd been asked to take a look at him, even though I knew next to nothing about horses.

Waiting for me that day was a rancher named Marty—the kind of man who looked like he'd been carved from sun and dust. As I stepped into the stable, he leaned against a wooden beam, chewing on a piece of hay.

"Horses don't lie, Doc," he said, watching me place my hands on Stoney's back. "They don't fake pain. They don't pretend to be fine when they're not. They tell you everything—if you know how to listen."

So, I began to listen.

Over the next several months, I learned to read Stoney's body like a language. The slope of his shoulders, the flick of his ears, the subtle shift of his weight—it all meant something. He never used words, but he was always communicating. And guiding me through it all was Marty.

He didn't teach with lectures or instructions. He taught by example—steady, watchful, patient. Marty had spent a lifetime with horses, not just riding them, but understanding them. He carried a quiet reverence for the mind of the horse, a deep respect for how they moved through the world—guided by instinct, energy, and trust.

His compassion wasn't loud, but it was unmistakable—shaped by decades of listening to beings that couldn't lie, and never asked for more than presence and respect.

Without realizing it, Marty passed down something far more valuable than technique.

He gave me a new way of seeing, of listening with my whole body, of honoring the truth of another being without trying to control it.

His wisdom had been earned over time. I was just beginning to grasp it.

Neither of us could've known how that wisdom would shape the way I would one day see people—their pain, their patterns, their nervous systems.

Or how what he gave me in that dusty barn would ripple far beyond the round pen—into classrooms, clinics, families, and lives.

The Language of Movement

I didn't listen to Stoney with my ears. I listened with my eyes—with stillness, attention, and presence. I observed first, without rushing to fix. Only then did I bring in logic—not to override what his body was telling me, but to understand it. Logic became a tool to honor the patterns I was seeing, not to control them.

Stoney spoke through movement. His nervous system responded instantly—to a shift in the wind, a flicker of emotion, the energy of the person beside him. There was no filter. No hesitation. He felt, and he reacted. His body told the truth.

And what I learned from him was simple but profound: Regulation doesn't begin in the mind. It starts in the body. Rhythm, movement, and safety aren't luxuries—they're the language of healing. And if we're willing to listen at that level, we'll always know where to begin.

Adam, I realized, was no different. He didn't need to be calmed down. He needed his nervous system to find its own rhythm. So we moved.

The Hike That Changed Everything

Walking wasn't enough. Adam's body still screamed with restless energy. So we hiked—up trails, through dirt paths, over uneven ground. I walked beside him, matching his pace, letting his body set the rhythm.

I didn't try to force eye contact. I didn't try to control him. I just observed. I watched his gait, his posture, the way his hands tensed and released. I noticed how he reacted to textures underfoot, how his breath changed with movement. His body was telling me a story.

And then something unexpected happened. A low hum filled the air.

Bees.

My pulse slammed in my ears. My chest tightened. I'm not mildly allergic—I'm anaphylactic. And there we were, miles from safety, no cell phone, and a swarm closing in. Panic kicked in. My body froze. I scanned the trail, searching for a way out.

But before I could react—before I could pull Adam away—he did something that stopped me cold. He crouched beside me, gently pressed his arm around my shoulder, and smiled.

Not fear. Not panic.

Calm.

The hum of the bees—the vibration—was regulating his sensory system. What should have overwhelmed him was, in that moment, organizing. And me? I was the one dysregulated. My nervous system was spiraling into freeze mode.

Adam—who had spent his life in a storm of sensory chaos—was the one grounding me.

The bees passed. My breath slowed. And when I looked at Adam—really looked—I knew something had shifted. His breath, once shallow and erratic, now moved steadily through his body. His hands, once clenched, now rested open and relaxed.

It wasn't a mindset shift. It wasn't a conscious decision.

His body had changed—and his brain followed.

The Body Leads

Your brain only knows the world through your body.

It doesn't see the world directly. It doesn't feel your emotions or read your experiences firsthand. It relies entirely on the signals your body sends it—moment by moment, breath by breath.

When your body feels tense, unsafe, or overstimulated, your brain assumes the world is dangerous—even if everything looks fine on the outside.

When your body feels calm, grounded, and supported, your brain interprets the world as safe. That's when clarity, connection, and healing become possible. This is why we can't think our way out of stress, trauma, or anxiety.

Because the brain isn't leading, it's responding.

The Missing Link

That moment with Adam sent me back to the foundations of neural development—to the early movement patterns that build the architecture of the nervous system.

Rolling. Crawling. Standing. Walking.

These weren't just childhood milestones. They were blueprints for regulation, connection, and safety. And when those patterns are skipped or disrupted, the nervous system adapts—but not always in helpful ways.

Symptoms like hyperactivity, inattention, emotional flooding—they're not failures. They're adaptations. I believed Adam's movement held the key to his transformation.

So I stopped trying to get him to focus harder or sit still longer.

I stopped chasing behaviors, and started following his body.

I guided him through simple, developmentally-rooted movements—not to train obedience, but to awaken dormant neural connections.

And his system responded. Not through force. Not through compliance.

But through his body's innate ability to reorganize and heal, when given the right input.

The Paradigm Shift

Adam's breakthrough didn't come from hours of talk therapy. It didn't come from new medications. It didn't come from trying to "fix" his mind. It came from rewiring his nervous system through movement.

And that truth doesn't just apply to children; It applies to all of us.

Because neuroplasticity—the brain's ability to change and rewire—isn't something we outgrow. It's built into our design. When we start with the body, the brain follows.

That became the foundation of everything I would go on to build.

INTRODUCTION

Why This Book Matters

We are living through a mental health crisis. Rates of anxiety, ADHD, and burnout are rising across every age group. People are overwhelmed, overstimulated, and emotionally flooded, despite having access to more tools, therapy, and wellness advice than ever before. They're doing everything "right": reading the books, practicing mindfulness, taking medication, and showing up for therapy yet still feeling stuck.

Why?

Because most approaches start in the wrong place. We've been told that if we can think better, we'll feel better. That if we reframe our thoughts, regulate our emotions, or develop better habits, we'll find peace. But these strategies assume something crucial: that the nervous system is already calm enough to cooperate.

What no one tells you is this:

You can't outthink a body that believes it's under threat. You can't focus, connect, or self-regulate when your nervous system is stuck in fight, flight, or freeze. Your brain might know you're safe, but if your body doesn't agree, your system won't respond.

This book exists to close that gap.

It introduces a new, science-backed approach to mental health. One that starts where your brain starts: the body. The Costello Method is a body-first framework for nervous system regulation, built on developmental movement, sensory processing, and the neuroscience of safety.

This isn't about coping harder. It's about retraining the signals your body sends to your brain. That way, regulation becomes your baseline, not your battle.

When you shift the input, everything changes:

- Focus becomes easier because your brain isn't stuck in defense.
- Emotional resilience returns because your system feels safe again.
- Recovery from stress happens naturally—not through willpower, but through wiring.

This book is for anyone who has tried to "fix" their mental health from the top down—and is ready to try something radically different.

Over the coming chapters, you'll learn:

- Why traditional approaches so often fall short—even when they're well-intentioned.
- How the nervous system creates—and resolves—patterns of anxiety, shutdown, and dysregulation.
- How to use movement to rewire your brain's stress response and build lasting emotional stability.

Whether you're navigating ADHD, burnout, trauma, or chronic anxiety—or supporting someone who is—this book will give you the tools to understand what's really happening beneath the surface. More importantly, it will help you create a system that knows how to come back to balance, on its own.

Because healing doesn't start with your thoughts. It starts with the signals your body sends every moment of every day.

And in the final section of this book, we'll take one more step, looking not just at symptoms, but at the labels themselves. We'll reframe traits like anxiety, ADHD, autism, and burnout not as fixed identities, but as nervous system patterns shaped by survival.

And when those patterns shift—so does everything else.

PART I

THE BODY HAS ALWAYS BEEN THE MISSING PIECE

Most people try to heal from the top down. They reflect, reframe, and reason their way through discomfort. And when it doesn't work, they assume they're doing it wrong—that they need more discipline, more insight, more control. But the nervous system doesn't respond to thought alone. It responds to input—through the body.

This is where we begin. Not with mindset, but with the system that holds it.

You'll meet people who are clear thinkers and deep feelers, often the ones others turn to for advice. They're highly self-aware. They can explain their patterns, name their triggers, and walk others through emotional storms.

And still, under pressure, their own systems spiral. They dissociate mid-conversation. They freeze when overwhelmed. They wake up already bracing for the day ahead. Not because they're broken—but because their bodies have never been shown another way.

This part isn't about more strategies. It's about returning to the foundation—where reflexes, rhythm, and regulation begin.

Because the truth is, you don't need more tools. You need a system that can use them.

So we start here, with a different kind of question. One that shifts the story from struggle to signal: Who really owns mental health?

CHAPTER 1

WHO OWNS MENTAL HEALTH?

Michael walked into my office carrying a kind of quiet pressure. Not frantic. Not collapsed. Just... clenched. His shirt was crisp. His posture upright. Every word he spoke landed with precision.

"I've done everything," he said, rubbing his temples. "Journaling. Breath work. Tracking my triggers. I can name exactly what's happening when it happens. But no matter how much I know, my body still hijacks the moment."

He wasn't confused. He wasn't in denial. He was exhausted from trying to out-think what his body kept overriding.

Michael could dissect his emotional patterns like a researcher. He was articulate. Emotionally literate. Disciplined. But none of it stopped the rush in his chest. The tension in his jaw. The breath that never dropped past his collarbones.

He didn't unravel. He withdrew. His nervous system didn't explode—it folded in on itself. Bracing. Scanning. Managing. And then, like so many, he judged himself for not being "better." You should be past this. You know what this is. Why is this still happening?

Michael wasn't missing the insight. He was missing access.

The Question Beneath the Question

What he was really asking, without saying it directly, was the question I've heard over and over again: Who owns mental health? Is it the mind? The brain? The will? Is it something we think our way into—or something our body must learn to access?

For decades, we've handed that question to disciplines and diagnoses. To medication, to mindset, to behavior strategies. Each approach claiming the solution lived in its lane.

But here we are—more therapy. More diagnoses. More self-help tools than ever before. And still, anxiety, ADHD, burnout, and emotional shutdown are on the rise.

Why? Because most of our solutions start at the top. This is known as a top-down approach: starting with the brain to influence the body. These strategies aim to adjust what you think, without first understanding how your system feels. But when your nervous system is already activated, it often needs a bottom-up path instead—beginning with the body to signal safety to the brain.

The assumption is simple: if you can name the pattern, you can change the pattern. But what happens when your body is already reacting before your brain catches up?

That's where Michael lived. He could narrate his emotional process in real-time. But by the time his insight kicked in, his nervous system had already launched a full-body response. He wasn't resisting regulation. He was trying to do it from the wrong place.

The Mindset Myth

Psychology has long shaped how we approach mental health. Talk therapy. Mindfulness. CBT. For many, these tools offer relief, clarity, and healing. But for the high-insight clients, the analyzers, the thinkers, the feelers, cognition alone doesn't always reach the root. Sometimes, the shutdown happens before a thought forms and bracing arrives before awareness. Trying to reframe your way into calm is like trying to call the train back after it's already left the station. It's not that you're wrong—you're just no longer in the driver's seat.

Psychology helps us understand story, identity, and meaning. But it often assumes that the mind leads the body. And that's where we've been mistaken. Mental health isn't just cognitive.

It's biological. It's physiological. It's sensory. It's a full-body system—not a single thought.

Chemistry Isn't the Whole Picture

Then there's psychiatry. With its lens focused on neurotransmitters, medication, and brain chemistry. For some, that chemistry shift opens a door. Stability increases. Emotions soften. Function improves. But meds don't teach your body what safety feels like. They don't rewire how your breath behaves in conflict. They don't change how your system responds to noise, interruption, or unpredictability.

Clients tell me, "I feel more functional... but I still don't feel like me." That's the line we keep walking—managing symptoms without restoring coherence. Reducing distress without rebuilding capacity.

The Performance Trap

Then there's the high-functioning wellness world. The self-optimizers. The breath-stackers. The cold plungers and time-blockers. They've got the tech, the discipline, and the data. But if the nervous system is braced, none of it sticks. You can't out-perform dysregulation. You can't optimize your way out of shutdown.

You can meditate—and still stay locked in hypervigilance. You can journal—and still brace every time your phone rings. Because healing isn't about how many tools you use. It's about how your body receives them.

What Michael Really Needed

Michael didn't need more insight. He needed to stop fighting his biology. To stop treating his tension as a failure. And start reading it as a signal. We didn't fix it in one session. But we started to listen differently.

And something shifted. His voice softened. His posture dropped. His breath deepened—just slightly. It wasn't resolution. It was recognition. And sometimes, that's the first form of repair.

So... who owns mental health?

The old model says: the brain. The mind. The story. The will. But if you've ever felt your system hijack a moment your brain understood— you know that's not the full story. Mental health doesn't start in the brain. It starts in the body: in the reflexes, the posture, the breath. In the subtle cues your system reads long before your thoughts catch up.

Where This Book Begins

The Costello Method starts at the foundation. Before mindset. Before motivation. Before narrative. With the body. Because it's your body that tells your brain what's safe. What's possible. What's available.

We'll explore how movement, rhythm, posture, and pressure shape your internal state. How you can train regulation, just like you train strength. And how your system isn't broken—it's simply waiting for the right input.

This isn't a book about trying harder. It's about remembering what your body already knows, and learning to trust it again.

Pause & Notice

- Does your chest tighten before your mind knows why?
- Do you feel like your mind "knows better," but your reactions still take over?
- Do you try tool after tool, yet still feel like you're bracing inside your skin?

You don't need more insight. You need access. And when your body feels safe—your mind can finally catch up.

Key Takeaways

Mental health isn't just a mindset—it's a full-body state shaped by regulation, not just reflection. Insight is powerful, but when the nervous system is bracing, knowledge alone can't bring change. This chapter reframes mental health not as something we think our way into, but something we access through the body.

Cognitive tools can bring clarity, perspective, and relief. But for people who understand their patterns—who can name what's happening but still feel swept up in the moment—those tools often land too late. You can't reframe your way out of a system that's still bracing. First, the body needs to feel safe. Only then can the mind truly respond.

Regulation isn't about mastering the mind. It's about reconnecting to the body—through movement, breath, rhythm, and awareness. When the body leads, the brain can follow. Like Michael, you're not missing insight. You're missing access.

CHAPTER 2

YOUR BRAIN HAS NEVER TOUCHED THE WORLD

Jason didn't walk into my office looking overwhelmed. He was steady. Quiet. One of those people who seemed like they'd already run the diagnostics on themselves.

"I've read the books," he said. "I know my patterns. But it still happens. The shift. It's like I'm fine, and then I'm not."

He couldn't name a trigger. There was no big event. Just a subtle unraveling he could feel, but not trace.

"I feel it in my gut first. Like something tightens. My breath pulls up. And then my mind catches up... like, oh, we're panicking now."

Jason wasn't lacking insight. He had the tools, the language, and awareness. But his body was running its own program—one that didn't wait for permission from his mind. That's what so many people miss. The brain doesn't make the first move. It responds to the messages the body sends. And when those messages are scrambled by pain, pressure, tension, or even a history of bracing, the brain doesn't pause to double-check.

It reacts and protects. It prepares for danger that may not even be there. That's not overreacting. That's how our system was built.

The Brain Lives in the Dark

Your brain has never seen the world. It's sealed inside your skull, cut off from the light, the wind, the sun, the voices around you. Everything it knows—everything it predicts, processes, or plans—it knows because of what your body tells it. Your heartbeat. Your breath. Your muscle tone. The way your feet touch the ground.

That's how your brain decides: Am I safe? Do I need to respond? Can I rest?

Mental health doesn't start in your thoughts. It starts in the signals underneath them.

When the Body Sends the Wrong Message

If your body is calm, your brain relaxes. If your body is tight, shallow, off-balance, or disoriented, your brain doesn't ask for context. It starts preparing.

That's the mistake we keep making—treating anxiety, burnout, and overwhelm as thought problems, when they're actually signal problems.

Jason didn't have a cognitive block. He had a gut-brain loop that had been firing danger signals for years. He had IBS. Abdominal tension. Shallow breathing. His body lived in a state of preemptive defense—so his brain stayed ready, even when life was quiet.

We didn't start with meditation. We started with motion. He learned how to move his diaphragm again. How to rock side to side until his brain stopped scanning for threat. How to anchor his feet to the floor, so his mind didn't have to float.

And the panic? It didn't vanish overnight. But it stopped arriving unannounced. Not because he changed his thoughts—but because his body started sending something new.

How Your Body Talks to Your Brain

Your body doesn't speak in words. It speaks in rhythm, pattern, pressure, space. Here's how it communicates safety—or threat:

- The vagus nerve: your calm switch

This long nerve runs from your brainstem down through your chest, lungs, and belly. It's the circuit that says: You can settle now.

When activated, it slows your heart. Deepens your breath. Softens your muscles. It's your body's "exhale" signal. But when under active? You stay stuck in tension—even when there's nothing to tense about.

- The sympathetic nervous system: your internal alarm

This is your body's rapid-response team: fight, flight, freeze. It's essential in real danger. But when it stays on? You live in a constant state of subtle bracing. Can't focus. Can't sleep. Can't drop your shoulders. That's not mindset. That's a body that forgot how to stand down.

- Reflexes: the first language of regulation

Before you could speak, your body already knew how to respond. You startled. You grasped. You braced.

These primitive reflexes were your earliest tools for navigating the world —instinctive patterns designed to protect and prepare you. As your brain matured, these reflexes were meant to fade into the background.

But sometimes, they don't. And when they linger, they can shape the way your body reacts to stress, fear, and overwhelm long into adulthood. A startle reflex that never integrated might keep you flinching. A postural reflex stuck in limbo might keep your core unstable, and your brain confused.

You can't talk a reflex into calm. You have to move it into completion.

- Proprioception: your internal GPS

This is how your body knows where it is in space. When this system is strong, you feel anchored. When it's weak, your brain loses context. So it compensates by scanning. Overthinking. Hyper vigilance.

That's why movement patterns—like crawling, compression, or balancing—aren't just exercises. They're recalibrations.

- Breath and heart rhythm: the music your brain listens to

The most primal feedback loop you have. If your heart and breath move with rhythm, your brain hears calm. If they stutter, spike, or hold—your brain hears: something's wrong.

The body trains the rhythm. The rhythm trains the brain.

The Costello Method: Movement as Medicine

Everything we've explored so far leads to one thing: your nervous system can be rewired. The Costello Method uses targeted movement, rhythmic sequencing, and reflex integration to rebuild your internal signals—so your brain can stop guessing, and start trusting.

This isn't performance. It's recalibration.

You don't "think" your way into focus. You give your body the kind of movement that restores it. You don't chase clarity. You create the conditions that allow it to stay. You don't force calm. You train your system to remember how to return there.

This Isn't a Self-Help Hack

If you've tried all the mindset tools and still feel flooded, if you've worked on your beliefs and still can't settle, if your body reacts before your thoughts even arrive—that's not failure. That's a system asking for a different entry point. This is it.

Pause & Notice

- Do you ever feel anxious—but can't explain why?
- Does your body brace even when your mind says, "You're fine"?
- Do your thoughts feel foggy—even after you've rested?

- Have you done the mindset work... but still feel stuck?

But if we change the input... we change the outcome.

Key Takeaways

Your brain doesn't create your mental state—it interprets it. Long before thoughts arrive, your body is already speaking in breath, balance, and reflex.

If the body signals safety, the brain relaxes. If the body braces, the brain prepares for danger—even if none exists.

This is why anxiety, emotional reactivity, and cognitive fog often don't begin in your thoughts. They begin in your systems of orientation: the vagus nerve, the breath, proprioception, and the reflexes underneath your posture.

When those patterns are dysregulated, your brain isn't malfunctioning —it's responding.

The Costello Method begins here: with the body. Through targeted movement, rhythm, and sensory feedback, we restore the signals that shape perception. Recalibration might look like softer shoulders in conflict, steadier breath in traffic, or an easier pause before you speak.

This isn't about forcing calm. It's about creating the conditions where calm becomes possible.

You haven't failed the tools. You've just been starting in the wrong place. But now you know where to begin.

CHAPTER 3

WHEN THE BODY BUILDS SURVIVAL INSTEAD OF SAFETY

M aya didn't look like someone stuck in survival.

She was sharp. Organized. The kind of person who sent thank-you notes and showed up five minutes early.

"I've done the work," she said. "Therapy. Mindfulness. Trauma recovery. I understand what's happening... but I can't shift it."

Even her voice had that quality: measured, intentional, trying hard not to shake. But her body told a different story. She sat rigid, her breath shallow, shoulders high. Every time the air conditioner clicked on, her eyes flicked sideways. Not startled. Just ready. She wasn't falling apart. She was holding it all together. But barely.

"It's like I'm stuck inside a system that overreacts before I even know there's anything to react to."

And she was right. Her nervous system wasn't resisting calm. It simply didn't know how to return to it.

When Neuroplasticity Works Against You

You've probably heard that the brain is always changing. That's true. Every experience you have—every movement, interaction, or breath—

shapes your nervous system. This ability to rewire is called neuroplasticity. It's what makes healing possible.

But here's the part people miss: neuroplasticity doesn't care if the input is helpful or harmful. It just adapts. Chronic stress, trauma, missed developmental sequences? The system adjusts. It finds workarounds. It builds shortcuts that help you cope—but leave you fragile.

We call this maladaptive plasticity: when the brain learns to survive, but not to regulate.

The Cost of Coping Loops

When your system builds survival shortcuts, they show up like this:

- Hypervigilance—scanning the room, the tone, the silence.
- Emotional whiplash—exploding, then going numb.
- Cognitive fatigue—not because you're lazy, but because your brain is managing a thousand invisible variables.
- And tension as your baseline—even rest feels like work.

These aren't flaws. They're adaptations. Your brain didn't fail you. It saved you. But now, those same patterns are keeping you from feeling safe—when you finally are.

You've probably heard the phrase "trauma is stored in the body." It's a familiar way of making sense of what we feel—but what's actually happening is more precise, and more hopeful.

Trauma isn't trapped in your muscles or locked into tissue.

It's encoded in the rhythms, reflexes, and protective patterns your nervous system learned to keep you safe. What we often call "trauma in the body" is really a signal loop that never got resolved.

That loop shows up as overreaction, shutdown, or hypersensitivity—not because something's broken, but because your system still thinks it has to protect you.

And the same neuroplasticity that wired those patterns in the first place is what makes it possible to change them.

Your nervous system isn't stuck. It's signaling. And when you change the input, the system doesn't have to stay on high alert. It can finally settle.

What Trauma Really Does

Trauma isn't just the event—it's how the experience imprints on your nervous system. Even once the moment has passed, your nervous system can stay stuck in protection mode, keeping your body braced as if the threat is still present. This imprint shapes how you feel, move, and respond—often without you realizing why. You flinch at a loud noise, even when you're safe. You freeze when plans suddenly change, even if nothing bad is happening. You dissociate during conflict, even when the situation is low-stakes.

It's not the memory alone—it's the unresolved imprint. Until the nervous system gets the chance to reset, the body keeps reacting as if it's still in survival. These aren't overreactions. They're deeply wired protective responses. And with the right support, those patterns can change.

Why? Because trauma imprints and wires your nervous system to stay reactive to future input. It doesn't just live in your thoughts. It lives in how your body prepares for threat, even when none exists.

And once you're in survival mode, your prefrontal cortex—the part of the brain that handles logic, language, and calm—goes offline. No amount of reasoning can override a body still living in defense.

What Maya Didn't Know

Maya had been bracing since birth. She skipped crawling. Never really rolled. She was "bright but fidgety." Did well in school, but hated transitions. Needed everything just so—or she shut down.

No one ever asked about her early development. They just saw the overwhelm and gave it names: anxiety, rigidity, high-functioning. But her nervous system had missed foundational steps. And under stress, the scaffolding crumbled. Her brilliance remained—but her body never caught up.

That's what Maya was feeling. Not failure. Disconnection.

Movement Was the Missing Map

At first, it felt beneath her. She wanted insight—not crawling drills. But we didn't start with strategy. We started with rhythm. Rocking. Rolling. Breathing in sync with motion. Crawling forward and back, cross-body and slow. We weren't treating trauma—we were restoring the movements that regulation depends on, the ones she never fully developed.

And then, little by little, she changed. She didn't freeze when plans shifted. She stopped micromanaging her partner's tone. She could pause in the middle of conflict—and stay with herself. "I didn't pretend to be calm," she told me once. "I was calm." Not because she forced it, but because her body finally remembered how to get there.

The Hidden Cost of Skipped Milestones

Not all dysregulation comes from trauma. Sometimes, it comes from developmental delay. Rolling. Crawling. Spinning. Balancing.

These aren't just cute baby moments. They are the foundational coding for movement, regulation, attention, and coordination.

When skipped or rushed, the nervous system builds weak bridges. And under pressure? Those bridges break.

You might notice: disorientation in noisy rooms; trouble staying still without fidgeting; emotional flooding from minor changes; chronic discomfort in crowds, movement, or multitasking.

These aren't adult issues. They're developmental echoes. And the good news? They're not set in stone.

Rewiring Isn't About Effort—It's About Input

The same brain that adapted under stress can rewire with the right support.

This isn't about forcing calm or thinking your way into regulation. It's about giving your nervous system the inputs it was wired to expect—but never received.

Not intense workouts—but early developmental patterns like crawling, rocking, and rolling. These activate the circuits that safety is built on.

Revisiting these stage-related sequences recalibrates the systems that never quite finished wiring—or that got derailed by trauma later in life.

Movement becomes the language the nervous system understands, because these patterns are how it learned to organize itself in the first place.

Breath follows. Not just deep inhales, but rhythmic, vagus-activating breath that signals: you're safe now.

Sensory input—pressure, balance, grounding—helps the system re-map space, trust, and body awareness.

These aren't exercises. They're reminders. And when delivered in the right sequence, they help the system shift from reaction to restoration.

This isn't performance. It's repair. It's not about doing more—it's about finishing what your system never got to complete. And when you change the input, your nervous system doesn't have to fight for regulation anymore.

It just returns to it—because now it knows the way.

The Real Definition of Resilience

Maladaptive plasticity doesn't mean your system is broken—it means it adapted the best way it knew how. Now, it gets to adapt again—on purpose, with rhythm, with safety.

The Costello Method doesn't manage symptoms; it restores function. So instead of white-knuckling through triggers, you find yourself recovering faster, moving smoother, feeling steadier. You don't force regulation. You return to it—because your body finally knows the way.

Pause & Notice

- Have you ever reacted faster than your mind could explain?
- Do small shifts or interruptions feel disproportionately overwhelming?
- Do you feel like your system is constantly "on"—even when nothing's wrong?
- Did you skip developmental milestones like crawling or rolling?

Your nervous system may not be dysregulated because you're anxious, or weak. It may simply be running on a framework that never got finished.

Key Takeaways

Sometimes the body builds survival instead of safety—and that's not failure, it's function. Neuroplasticity doesn't judge input; it just adapts. If your system grew up in stress or skipped key developmental stages, it built coping loops that helped you get through. But those same loops can leave you fragile under pressure.

These patterns aren't signs of brokenness; they're brilliance in the face of unmet need. Trauma isn't just a memory—it's a reflex, a posture, a movement your body keeps rehearsing long after the threat is gone. And when foundational milestones like crawling, rolling, or balancing are skipped, the nervous system misses key wiring. Under stress, that scaffolding can collapse.

Healing doesn't happen by trying harder. It happens by giving the system the input it never got. Movement becomes medicine. Regulation becomes a memory your body can finally retrieve. And resilience? It's not a trait you force—it's a rhythm your system learns to return to, again and again.

CHAPTER 4

CORTEX VS. SUBCORTEX – WHO'S REALLY IN CHARGE?

It was just a ten-second ride. Ten floors. Familiar building. Nothing unusual. But the moment the elevator doors closed, my body made a decision. Heart pounding. Breath cutting sharp through my chest. Palms sweating. Every muscle bracing as if I were about to crash.

My cortex—the logical, knowing part of my brain—whispered, "You're fine. You've done this before." But that voice had no power anymore. My subcortex had already taken over.

"Nope," it said. "This is not safe. Prepare for impact."

And just like that, I was in it. Not a full-blown panic attack. Not a dramatic meltdown. Just a silent, precise storm—one my body had rehearsed too many times before. I wasn't choosing fear. I wasn't overreacting. I wasn't weak. My nervous system was doing exactly what it thought it was supposed to do.

When the Thinking Brain Isn't in Charge

You've probably felt it too. Your heart races before a meeting you're completely prepared for. You snap at your partner over something small —then wonder where it came from. You freeze in the middle of a conversation and can't explain why. These aren't failures of willpower. They're patterns of protection.

We're taught that if we're just aware enough, we can stay regulated. But awareness doesn't always reach the part of your brain that makes the first move. Because your cortex—the rational, reflective part of your mind—isn't the first responder. Your subcortex is.

And once that part is online? Your thinking brain gets quiet. Not because you lack control—but because your body is trying to keep you safe.

Two Brains, One Body

Think of your brain like a house with two floors. Upstairs lives the cortex—the CEO. It's thoughtful. Language-based. It handles planning, analysis, emotional regulation.

Downstairs is the subcortex—the first responder. It's fast. Automatic. It's where movement, reflexes, and survival patterns live. The subcortex doesn't wait for you to think. It reacts—to movement, to sound, to posture, to tone, to a subtle shift in breath or a perceived lack of space.

And if your cortex says, "It's fine," but your subcortex says, "This is a threat," guess who wins? The body always listens to the faster voice.

Jada's Red Light

Jada was a trauma therapist. Poised. Grounded. Skilled. She helped others regulate every single day. But by 5:30 p.m., she felt like someone else entirely.

"I can walk someone through panic at 10 a.m.," she told me, "and by rush hour, I'm gripping the wheel like my life depends on it."

Her trigger? Traffic. Not the inconvenience. The immobility. The pressure. The lack of exit. Her cortex knew she wasn't in danger. But her subcortex—her survival brain—had built a different map: tight space? No control? Must brace.

What changed for Jada wasn't mindset. It was movement. We added short, daily inputs: grounding drills in the morning, cross-body integration at lunch, paired breath and motion before driving home.

And something shifted. Her breath stayed low. Her jaw released. She didn't have to try to calm down—her body stayed calm by default. Not because the world changed. But because she did.

Why Your Body Reacts Before You Think

The subcortex stores memory in a different language. It doesn't speak in words. It speaks in posture, pressure, and rhythm.

That's why a tone can tighten your chest. A voice can freeze your breath. A scent or a space can flip your mood before you know why.

It's not emotional immaturity. It's not irrationality. It's a system operating on reflexes that formed long before your first conscious thought. And unless you speak its language—movement, breath, grounding— you can't reach it through logic.

Why Self-Talk Isn't Always Enough

You can't reframe a reaction that hasn't entered the realm of words yet. The nervous system listens to: muscle tone, gaze stability, breath patterns, sensory input, proprioception, and vestibular signals.

Saying, "You're safe" doesn't land if your jaw is clenched, your diaphragm is frozen, and your balance systems are dysregulated. It's like speaking English to a brain that only understands Morse code. What reaches the subcortex isn't thought. It's felt experience.

The Fastest Path to the Survival Brain? Movement

You can't talk the subcortex into safety. But you can show it. This is where bottom-up work begins. Not with affirmations. But with patterns that regulate the parts of you that don't speak in language. That includes:

Cross-body movements → reconnect hemispheres and stabilize sequencing

Reflex resets → interrupt survival loops that got stuck

Vagal activation → support the calm switch your body forgot how to use

Proprioceptive input → tell the brain where you are so it doesn't brace

Rhythmic motion → revisit the movement patterns your nervous system once used to build safety, connection, and co-regulation

Each rep says: You're here. You're okay. You don't need to run. And slowly, the subcortex begins to believe it.

Who's Actually Driving?

In everyday life, it's easy to assume your cortex is in charge. After all, it's the part that speaks. But in moments of stress, your subcortex holds the wheel. It decides if you bolt, freeze, rage, dissociate—or regulate.

And unless you've wired that system to stay steady, it will default to the same old loops: scan, brace, overcorrect, collapse.

But here's the hope: the subcortex isn't frozen in time. It's changeable. It's listening for something new, and movement is how you send the message.

You Can't Out-Think the Subcortex. But You Can Rewire It.

When you stop trying to override your nervous system with willpower... and start working with it through rhythm, reflex, and sensory regulation... you don't just get relief. You get capacity.

You don't just understand your stress. You move through it—without spiraling. You stop coaching your brain through chaos. And start wiring your system to meet it with steadiness.

Because when the subcortex stops bracing... your cortex can finally return. Not to save you. But to guide you.

Pause & Notice

- Do you ever feel like your reactions happen before your thoughts can catch up?

- Have you tried logic, mindfulness, or reframing—and still felt hijacked by emotion?
- Does your breath shift in crowds, conflict, or silence—even when you "know" you're okay?
- Do you want to be calm—but your body doesn't seem to get the memo?

The problem isn't your mindset. It's the input. And once your body starts receiving the right signals... regulation won't just feel possible—it will feel familiar.

Key Takeaways

Your thinking brain doesn't lead in moments of stress—your survival brain does. The subcortex is fast, automatic, and wired to protect. It reacts to posture, breath, space, and tone long before logic kicks in. That's why self-talk, insight, and awareness often fall short. They arrive too late.

You can't reason with a nervous system that's already bracing—you have to rewire it from the body up. Movement, rhythm, breath, and sensory input are the language the subcortex understands. When those signals are consistent, the system starts to believe it's safe again.

That's how regulation becomes possible—not through trying harder, but through showing your body something new. Because when the subcortex settles, the cortex can return—and you stop surviving and start responding.

CHAPTER 5

THE MYTH OF THINKING YOUR WAY TO REGULATION

Brenda was the kind of client who made me slow down. Not because she was falling apart. Not because she needed fixing. But because everything about her whispered effort, quiet, invisible effort. The kind that hides in good posture and polished sentences. That lives in the pause between answering a question and feeling it.

She arrived early. Took notes. Maintained steady eye contact. You could tell she'd done the work—years of therapy, self-study, and reflection. She wasn't chaotic or shut down. She was... hovering. Present, but not landed. In the room, but not quite in her body.

"I'm not overwhelmed," she said one day, "I'm just... not here. It's like I'm watching myself move through the day from a few feet away." She said it with calm clarity. But her breath never dropped below her collarbone.

Her shoulders were upright, but stiff. Her gaze was warm—but slightly misaligned, like she was monitoring herself from the inside. She wasn't dramatic. She wasn't in distress. She was disconnected. And her nervous system was doing exactly what it was designed to do.

Freeze Doesn't Always Look Like Crisis

Brenda didn't look frozen. She looked like a high-functioning adult who knew her patterns better than most practitioners. But freeze doesn't always knock you down. Sometimes it puts you on autopilot—quietly braced, outwardly composed, inwardly unreachable.

She could hold her job. Hold eye contact. Hold space for others. But she couldn't hold presence.

This wasn't dissociation in the classic sense. It was the kind that slips under the radar: a voice that sounds steady, but never soft; a breath that's present, but never full; a body that performs calm, but never feels it.

Her system wasn't malfunctioning. It was surviving. And for Brenda, survival meant stillness without safety.

That's what freeze is. Not collapse. Conservation. Not shutdown. Suspension. The world calls it composure. The body calls it compression.

When the Thinking Brain Is Offline

Brenda could name every pattern in clinical detail. She had language for her attachment style. She knew how her childhood wired her triggers. She could walk you through the neuroscience of stress response.

But knowledge didn't bring her home to herself.

Because freeze lives in the body—not the brain. And when the nervous system enters freeze, the cortex—the part of you that thinks, reflects, reframes—goes dim.

The very tools Brenda had mastered—mindfulness, journaling, cognitive reappraisal—required a system that was online. But her body kept logging off before she could use them.

She wasn't skipping her tools. Her system was simply... gone.

The Top-Down Trap

There's a myth that runs deep in mental health: "If I understand it, I can change it." But for people like Brenda, understanding isn't the problem —access is. When your body has learned that presence equals threat, it doesn't wait for your insight; it bypasses it, swiftly and silently.

By the time you try to calm your breath, your diaphragm has already locked. By the time you try to think clearly, your vision has already narrowed. By the time you try to stay, your body has already left. This isn't avoidance—it's adaptation.

The cortex can't lead if the subcortex has pulled the plug. And dysregulation doesn't care how many affirmations you've memorized.

Not Just Freeze – The Full Spectrum of Survival

Freeze often shows up quietly—in composure, in stillness, in numbness —but it's not the only survival state that hijacks regulation. Some people live in fight: always bracing, defensive, easily irritated. Others live in flight: overworking, overthinking, overdoing—never still, never settled. You might not shut down like Brenda; you might speed up. You might get sharper, louder, quicker to anger or escape.

That's not a personality trait—it's a nervous system trying to defend you with motion instead of stillness.

- **Fight says**: If I stay ready, I can't get hurt.
- **Flight says**: If I move fast enough, I can outrun the threat.
- **Freeze says**: If I disappear, nothing can reach me.

All of these are adaptations. All of them are intelligent. And none of them are sustainable.

When your system lives in defense, your brain can't lead.

That's why the Costello Method doesn't try to suppress these responses. It gives your body a safer option—through movement that signals "you're not under threat anymore."

This is not about controlling the mind. It's about sending the right cues to the system underneath it.

High Achievers: Calm Isn't a Character Trait—It's a Body State

This trap is especially familiar to high achievers—the executives, team leaders, caregivers, and clinicians who manage chaos with composure but feel hollow once the day ends. You perform regulation well, but performing calm isn't the same as feeling it. You may journal, meditate, and schedule your self-care to the minute—and still feel flat. Not because you're doing it wrong, but because your nervous system is still dysregulated, stuck in a loop of overdrive or collapse. Regulation isn't about controlling your output; it's about letting your input land. And when your system starts to feel safe in stillness—not just busy—you stop trying to manage your symptoms and begin to soften into yourself.

The Shift: From Trying to Trusting

We didn't start with mindset work. We didn't dive into inner child processing or narrative reconstruction.

We did something radical in its simplicity: we slowed down. Slower than she wanted. Slower than her achiever identity could tolerate. Slower than what felt "productive." And in that stillness, we watched.

We looked for flickers of return: a breath that reached her ribs, a glance that actually landed, a moment when her voice dropped an octave, a flicker of softness in her tone. No catharsis. No unraveling. Just quiet, repetitive invitations to stay.

Movement, rocking, compression, cross-body integration, and grounding drills reminded her: You're safe now. You don't have to float. And one day, she said it in passing: "I laughed in the car yesterday. Not at anything. Just... because I could. I didn't realize how much I'd missed that."

That's how dysregulation unwinds. Not with a breakthrough. But with a return. Not by force. But by rhythm.

Parents: Your Child Doesn't Need More Discipline—They Need a Signal

This process is also true for children—especially those who are neurodivergent. Parents often feel helpless watching their child spiral, even after therapy, visual schedules, and tools.

"They know what to do," they'll say. "But they still can't do it." That's not disobedience. It's dysregulation.

A child's nervous system may be in fight, flight, or freeze—zoning out, melting down, bolting, or clinging. What you're seeing isn't resistance. It's a system in overwhelm. In that moment, they're not ignoring your guidance. They've lost access to it.

No reasoning, reward chart, or timeout can override a system that's gone offline. But movement can. Rhythm can. Breath, pressure, and safety cues can. These are the tools we use in the Costello Method—and you can use them too.

Freeze Isn't Failure. It's a Nervous System in Conservation

If you've been carrying a sense of numbness—if you float through your day, functional but not quite in it; if you've done every journaling prompt, every meditation, every mindset shift, and still feel like your body and brain are out of sync—it's not because you're not trying hard enough. It might be because your system is still dysregulated. Not collapsed, just quietly withdrawn or caught in overdrive.

And here's the thing no one tells you: dysregulation doesn't respond to insight. It responds to signal. To consistency. To felt safety. And when the right input arrives, the body starts to come back. The breath drops. The tension unwinds. The presence returns—not as a goal, but as a byproduct of regulation.

Fitness Practitioners: Why Specific Movement Matters

If you're a coach, a dancer, a martial artist, or a lifelong mover—you already know movement affects mood.

What you may not realize is how intentional movement supports nervous system regulation. This isn't just about moving more. It's about moving intentionally.

- Jumping jacks stimulate the vestibular system and reawaken midline integration.
- Cross-body patterns like marching or crawling train hemispheric communication.
- Compression drills like squats or push-holds activate proprioceptive input that signals safety.
- Balancing trains the brain to map spatial context—critical when the world feels overwhelming.
- Rhythmic movement helps calm the amygdala by resetting the brain's stress loops.

This is why in the Costello Method, we don't guess. We sequence. Each movement targets a specific neural pathway—reflexive, sensory, integrative. We move to access the systems that mindset alone can't reach.

You don't have to abandon your training style. But when you bring intention to how movement speaks to the brain, your workout becomes more than a routine. It becomes regulation in action.

Why the Costello Method Begins with the Body

Because when the nervous system is dysregulated, the thinking brain can't take the lead. The Costello Method doesn't offer quick hacks for focus, clarity, or calm.

It restores the foundation those states rely on—by rebuilding the body-brain pathways that allow your brain to feel safe inside your body again.

We don't just talk about trauma—we unwind the reflexes it imprinted. We don't just name freeze—we gently melt it through rhythmic, regulating movement. This is the difference between managing symptoms and restoring connection.

Between holding yourself together... and finally being able to exhale.

What Comes Next

If Chapter 1 showed you where mental health really begins… and Chapter 2 introduced the body-brain conversation… this chapter is the bridge.

The point where we stop asking your brain to do all the work. And start building the conditions that allow it to rest. Because regulation isn't something you think your way into. It's something experienced, and your body already knows the way back.

Pause & Notice

- Do you find yourself present, but not in your body?
- Have you "done the work" but still feel flat, numb, or outside of yourself?
- Do you perform regulation better than you feel it?
- Do you know all the tools—but your body never quite catches up?

You're not missing anything. You've been protecting something. And now, your system is allowed to come back.

Key Takeaways

Dysregulation doesn't always look like chaos. Sometimes it looks like composure, or control. Insight alone can't bring your system back online—and that's not a failure of effort; it's a signal for a new approach. You can't override survival patterns with strategy; you have to reach them with rhythm.

That's why the Costello Method doesn't start with thought work—it starts with the body. Breath. Rocking. Grounding. Movement that sends the message: it's safe to land now. When the system feels safe, presence returns—not as a performance, but as a byproduct of connection. You don't have to perform calm—you get to feel it.

CHAPTER 6
WHAT KEEPS YOU STUCK

Many people reach this point knowing exactly what's wrong—and still feel stuck. They've done the work. Built the toolkit. Practiced the strategies. But their system doesn't shift. That's not a failure of willpower. It's a reflection of how the nervous system works.

Diana was one of those people.

The Moment It Shifted

I still remember the moment Diana walked into my office. She moved like someone who didn't have time to waste—every step, every glance, every breath had a mission. She was already mid-sentence before she sat down—apologizing for being early, adjusting her ponytail, checking her Apple Watch like it was part of her nervous system.

From the outside, she was magnetic. Capable. Controlled. Charismatic. The kind of person who's never behind. The one others lean on. Smart. Sharp. Structured.

"I'm not burned out," she said. "I just feel... off. I'm doing everything right. But my runs are slower, my brain feels foggy, and I keep waking up tired."

She didn't look like someone in survival mode—she looked like someone in performance mode.

Morning workouts. Evening meditations. HRV tracking. Her supplement routine was dialed in, down to the hour. She could quote her therapist and her lab results in the same breath.

"If I stop moving," she said, "everything catches up with me—and not in a good way."

She looked strong. She was strong. But my nervous system caught something hers hadn't named yet. Her breath never dropped below her collarbones. Her posture was upright, but never at ease. Even her stillness felt effortful.

"I'm not avoiding stress," she said. "I'm attacking it."

That's when I knew: her discipline wasn't helping her feel safe. It was helping her stay in control.

When Regulation Becomes a Performance

To most people, Diana looked like the picture of nervous system mastery. She was emotionally articulate. On time. On point.

But regulation isn't how you look. It's how you recover. And Diana's system couldn't. She told me rest made her restless. That vacations drained her more than work. That she could sit through yin yoga—but her mind spun the whole time.

"Stillness makes me feel like I'm disappearing," she said. "So I just keep moving."

Maybe you know that feeling too. That sense that if you slow down—even for a second—everything you've been holding back will catch up to you. So you stay in motion. Not to heal. But to outrun.

That was Diana's version of dysregulation: not chaotic, but constantly doing. A nervous system locked in a rhythm of effort.

This kind of dysregulation gets missed all the time—because it doesn't collapse.

It over-functions. It organizes. It holds space for others. Until it can't.

Insight Without Access

Diana had insight. She knew her patterns. She could name them in real time.

"I can tell you the exact moment I go into overdrive," she said. "I just can't stop it."

She wasn't stuck because she lacked awareness. She was stuck because awareness came too late.

By the time she reached for a tool, her breath had already shortened. Her body had already braced. Her nervous system had already made its decision—and her brain was trying to catch up.

If that feels familiar—if you've done the work, built the toolkit, tracked the patterns—and still feel hijacked...

That's not a failure of effort. That's a nervous system doing exactly what it learned to do. You can have all the insight in the world—but if your body doesn't have access, nothing shifts.

When Movement Misses the Message

When therapy plateaued, Diana leaned harder into movement. Running. Lifting. Yoga. More output. More structure. It worked—until it didn't.

"If I don't move," she said, "I feel like I'll explode. Or crash. Or both."

Not all movement heals. Some movement rehearses the very stress patterns we're trying to undo. Diana's body wasn't recovering. It was rehearsing stress. She wasn't relaxing through movement. She was surviving through it.

Changing the Conversation With Her Body

Diana didn't need less movement. She needed a different relationship with it.

. . .

So we shifted the goal:

Rhythm instead of reps.

Coordination instead of control.

Breath-led movement instead of performance output.

We introduced vestibular resets, cross-body drills—slower, simpler patterns that signaled familiarity and safety rather than pushing capacity.

She didn't need to tell her body it was safe. She needed to show it. And that kind of belief doesn't come from thought. It comes from repetition. Not more effort—just a different input.

When Healing Becomes Just Another Project

At one point, Diana went all in: cold plunges, fasting, caffeine detox, cardio doubles, and journaling.

"If I can just get ahead of it," she said, "maybe I can finally stop feeling like this."

Maybe you've had that moment too—where healing becomes a checklist. As if you could spreadsheet your way to safety. Where wellness starts to feel like a job. But healing isn't a productivity project. And when your system is already in survival mode, even "healthy" habits can feel like a threat.

Within two weeks, her sleep tanked. Her anxiety spiked. She felt worse than when she started. Not because she failed, but because her system was flooded. She wasn't doing it wrong. She was just doing too much—for a body that was already bracing.

Where We Left Off

We didn't take everything away. We traded volume for tempo. Bracing for breath. Effort for rhythm. Movement became a way to find ease again—not to prove capacity. A few weeks in, she said something I'll never forget:

"I went for a walk last night. No podcast. No goal. I just walked.

And for the first time, I wasn't trying to escape anything.

I just felt... okay."

Not fixed. Not finished. Just beginning to trust that safety didn't have to be earned.

The Pattern Beneath the Progress

Diana's story isn't rare. I've seen it over and over—high-functioning, high-capacity, well-resourced people doing everything right, and still feeling stuck. Not because they're broken, but because they're trying to heal using the same tools that taught them to override: discipline, optimization, effort. But regulation doesn't come through performance.

It comes through pattern. Through rhythm. Through repetition. Through breath. That's how the nervous system learns to settle. That's how we begin to rewire—not by force, but by design. And that's how we finally start to get unstuck.

Pause & Notice

- Do you feel restless when you try to slow down?
- Does stillness make you anxious—like you're falling behind?
- Do you find yourself treating healing like another project to optimize?
- Does movement help you feel better—or just help you stay in control?

You're not overdoing it because you're flawed. You may be overdoing it because your nervous system is still wired for urgency—and hasn't felt safe enough to slow down.

Key Takeaways

Not all dysregulation looks like falling apart. Sometimes it looks like high performance: structure, discipline, movement, insight.

But underneath all that effort, the nervous system may still be bracing—not out of failure, but out of habit.

Diana wasn't stuck because she didn't know enough. She was stuck because her system never had a chance to feel safe without effort.

When healing becomes another project to optimize, the body doesn't relax—it resists. Not because it's broken, but because the input feels familiar—not restorative. This chapter is a reminder that even the most resourced, insightful people can still feel hijacked by their own system. Not because they're doing it wrong—but because regulation doesn't happen through force.

It happens through rhythm. Repetition. Breath. These are patterns that signal: You don't have to keep pushing.

Healing isn't something you earn.

It's something your body remembers—when it finally feels safe enough to stop performing.

PART II
WHERE REGULATION BEGINS

You've made it through the first part of the story, the part where most healing journeys begin and, unfortunately, get stuck. You've seen why insight alone can't open the door. Why knowing your patterns doesn't always change them. Why mindset, no matter how sharp, can't lead a system that's still bracing. Now we begin the work that shifts everything.

This part introduces you to the Costello Method, a body-first, brain-informed framework that doesn't just talk about healing. It shows your system how to live it. Not through hacks. Not through pressure. But through rhythm, movement, and a language your nervous system already understands.

These chapters are where theory becomes felt experience. Where reflexes begin to integrate. Where regulation stops being a concept, and starts becoming something your body can hold.

We'll start with the soft signs—the ones you may have dismissed or worked around for years: the tension you can't shake. The energy crashes. The zoning out. The need to fidget or brace or micromanage every moment just to get through the day. These aren't flaws. They're messages. What if your body wasn't betraying you... but trying to guide you back?

Because the body doesn't need to be talked into change. It just needs the right input. You don't need more willpower. You don't need to try harder. You need a different starting point: one that begins below thought.

By the end of this section, you won't just understand the nervous system. You'll know how to work with it. And more importantly, you'll know how to listen to the part of you that's been speaking all along.

Let's begin—not with force, but with something softer. Let's begin with what your body's been waiting for.

CHAPTER 7
WHAT YOUR BODY IS TELLING YOU

L ong before there's a diagnosis—before burnout, anxiety, or trauma has a name—your body knows. It speaks in small ways. Subtle shifts. Flickers of tension. Startles that never quite settle.

This chapter is about those early, often-overlooked signals. Not pathology. Not prediction. But patterns; signs your nervous system is working overtime just to keep you upright. Clinically, we call them neurological soft signs—subtle, body-based cues that don't show up on tests, but speak volumes about how regulated or dysregulated your system really is.

Take Ava. She was the kind of person who tried. She journaled. She meditated. She did breathe work every night before bed. She read all the books, followed the protocols, and practiced every regulation tip she could find. But her body told a different story.

Her shoulders stayed lifted, like they were bracing for bad news. Her jaw ached in the mornings. Loud noises made her flinch—sometimes even the clink of silverware sent a jolt through her chest.

At first, she brushed it off. Tension habits. Personality stuff. Just how she was wired. But the more we slowed things down, the clearer it became: these weren't quirks. They were messages. Her body had been speaking all along. No one had taught her how to listen.

Your Body Is Always Talking

If you've ever felt "on" even when your mind is trying to slow down. If people have called you fidgety, sensitive, or "too much"... If you've chalked up your tension to personality or stress—Your system is doing exactly what it was designed to do. You're reading signals no one taught you to understand.

Your nervous system doesn't just speak through thoughts or feelings. It speaks through rhythm, reflex, posture, and breath. When those signals get ignored or misread, you feel off—but can't explain why. You feel too much. Or feel nothing at all. You look fine on the outside, while your system works silently in overdrive.

This chapter is here to decode that language. Not to label you. But to help you recognize that what you've called "just who I am" might actually be: a system asking for support.

What Are Neurological Soft Signs?

They're subtle, body-based signals that show where your nervous system is struggling to regulate. Not dramatic. But real.

These signs don't show up on tests. But they show up in your life.

- Shoulders that never drop
- Jaw clenching until it hurts
- Jumping at small sounds
- Tripping over nothing
- Struggling to sit still or stay focused
- Feeling overwhelmed in crowds

These aren't flaws. They're compensations—your brain's best attempt to work around what never got fully wired. And once you understand them, they stop feeling random. They start showing you the way back.

Ava's Nervous System Was Speaking Loudly

Ava had always considered herself "type A." Sharp. Productive. Slightly anxious, but high functioning. She never stopped moving—and no one expected her to. But underneath all that forward motion was a body stuck in survival.

She didn't collapse. She coped. But the cost was high. Constant tension. Restless energy. Sensory overload. Things that didn't seem like a big deal, until they added up to exhaustion.

When we slowed down, she began noticing what her body was doing without her consent: her shoulders would rise every time she tried to relax. Her legs bounced through meetings. Her breath stayed tight and shallow—even during meditation.

Therapy gave her language. Mindfulness gave her awareness. But neither gave her access. Why? Because her patterns weren't rooted in thought. They were wired into reflexes, posture, and sensory processing.

Once we introduced body-first input—movement to regulate her vestibular system and integrate postural reflexes—everything shifted. She stopped trying to relax. Her body just did it. She stopped flinching. She slept deeper. Her mind felt quieter—not because she tried harder, but because her system no longer felt under threat. Ava hadn't failed to regulate. She'd just been trying to enter through the wrong door.

The Most Common Signs You're Missing

When I began tracking nervous system patterns, I saw the same signs repeat—quiet, consistent, and misunderstood. If you've lived with any of these, you're not imagining it:

- Shoulders tension, even at rest
- A jaw that clenches before you notice
- Restlessness
- Fidgeting, body shifting constantly
- Overwhelm in crowds,
- Irritated by bright lights, or noisy spaces

- Struggling to read
- Difficulty staying focused
- Feeling clumsy and off-balance

These aren't personality traits. They're nervous system signals. They tell the story of a body that's working too hard just to feel okay.

The High Performer with Hidden Dysregulation

Michael was sharp. Strategic. Driven. He ran a company, traveled often, and made quick decisions under pressure. But his body was telling a different story.

He startled at Slack pings. He bumped into doorframes and tripped on curbs. He fidgeted constantly—even when he was "relaxing."

He chalked it up to stress. But when we looked closer, it was clear: his vestibular and proprioceptive systems were out of sync. His reflexes were unintegrated. His body was bracing—all day long.

Once we gave his system the input it was missing—rhythmic movement, balance drills, pressure and rotation—his body recalibrated. The flinching stopped. His posture adjusted. His mind felt clearer. He didn't change his life. He changed the way his body sensed it. That's the power of nervous system-based work.

The Physiology Beneath the Patterns

Let's break down what these soft signs actually reflect:

The Brainstem – Always On Alert

When this system is under strain, your body stays braced. Tension builds. Breath stays shallow. Small stressors feel huge.

The Vestibular System – Motion and Balance

It's the system that helps your brain track motion, stillness, and gravity. When it's off, you don't just feel dizzy—you feel disoriented. Foggy. Unsettled. Even when everything around you is still.

. . .

Proprioception – Where You Are in Space

This is your internal GPS. When it's weak, you feel disconnected, clumsy, or ungrounded. You fidget not because you're distracted—but because your body's searching for feedback.

Hemispheric Integration – Whole-Brain Access

When the left and right sides of your brain aren't working together, you struggle to read smoothly, stay focused, or shift gears. Your system compensates—and life just feels harder than it should.

If you've been carrying these signs quietly, chalking them up to stress or sensitivity—hear this: It's not weakness, it's wiring. You're adaptive. Your nervous system learned to survive. Now it needs help learning how to settle.

Where We Go From Here

Recognizing soft signs is a powerful first step. But insight alone isn't enough to shift the system. Many people get stuck here—aware of their patterns, but unable to change them. They try harder. Move more. Meditate more. Push through the overwhelm. But regulation doesn't come from effort. It comes from input.

In the next chapter, you'll meet someone who did everything "right"— and still couldn't settle. Their story will help us uncover what it really takes to build lasting regulation—and how the Costello Method helps the body remember what safety actually feels like.

Once you understand these soft signs for what they are—calls for input, not effort—you can start to learn how to respond to them in the way your body actually needs. Because you don't have to fight your way into calm. You just have to create the conditions that let it return.

Pause & Notice

- Do you carry tension even when you're trying to relax?

- Do your shoulders stay high, your breath shallow—even during meditation?
- Have you dismissed clumsiness, or sensory sensitivity as "just how I am"?
- Does your body feel wired—even when your mind wants to be still?
- Do you flinch at small sounds or feel overstimulated in crowds?

You're not too sensitive. You might just be carrying signals your nervous system hasn't had the right input to resolve—yet.

Key Takeaways

Sometimes, dysregulation doesn't look like panic. It looks like effort. Quiet, invisible effort—just to get through the day.

Your body might be bracing in ways you've never noticed. A jaw that tenses overnight. Shoulders that rise when you try to rest. A breath that won't drop below your chest. These aren't flaws. They're signals.

They're the body's way of saying, "I'm trying. But I don't feel safe yet."

You don't need to override these patterns. You need to understand them. Because once you stop calling them quirks or personality, you can start responding to what they really are: unmet needs from your nervous system.

And the good news?

You don't have to figure it out. You just have to feed the system what it's been missing—movement, rhythm, input. Regulation doesn't come from effort. It comes from access. And once your system has that access, the tension doesn't have to be managed anymore.

It just lets go.

CHAPTER 8

THE COSTELLO METHOD – MOVEMENT WITH A PURPOSE

U p to now, you've explored *what's* happening in your system. Now, we shift into *how to work with it*. Because healing isn't about trying harder. It's about giving your body the right input, in the right order, so it can remember what safety feels like.

This is where insight becomes action. Where your nervous system stops being the barrier and starts becoming the guide.

The Moment It Shifted

I started noticing a pattern. Clients were showing up with full toolkits. They had the language. The commitment. The insight. Some had been in therapy for years. Others were just starting their journey. Still, they were deeply self-aware. Many were the "strong ones"—the ones others leaned on. Therapists. Teachers. Parents of neurodivergent kids. Coaches. Nurses. People who knew how to do the work. They were tracking, breathing, meditating—doing everything they'd been told would help. They could name their attachment style mid-conflict. But their breath was still shallow. Their shoulders were still braced. Their eyes still scanned for exits, even in safe rooms. One client said something I'll never forget: "I know this is my stress response... but it feels like my body reacts before I even get a vote." That wasn't an outlier. That was the pattern.

When Effort Stops Working

I started seeing two groups—on opposite ends of the spectrum. Some were pushing through hyper-disciplined routines: training five days a week, tracking every metric. Not avoiding discomfort, but chasing it. Hoping that if they moved fast enough, worked hard enough, they'd finally feel calm. But the calm never came. Others weren't moving at all, not because they didn't care, but because movement felt foreign. Unsafe. Disorienting. Stillness made them anxious and effort made them exhausted.

It might sound contradictory. Yet both were symptoms of the same thing: a system stuck in dysregulation. The problem wasn't mindset. It was Neuroception—the body's built-in radar for safety and threat. Their systems had learned: movement equals danger, stillness equals exposure. They weren't resisting healing. They were bracing for it. And across both ends of the spectrum, I kept hearing the same quiet question: "Why isn't this working?"

High Performers Aren't Broken. They're Braced

This isn't just the question of people in visible distress. It's the quiet confusion of high performers, caregivers, and clinicians. The ones who rarely collapse, but never quite relax. The ones who manage deadlines, care for others, do all the "right things," and still feel wired, flat, or like they're always slightly bracing for something. They've read the books. Tracked their habits. Tried the breath work and the meditation and the mindfulness app.

You're not skipping steps. You're just stuck in a system that doesn't shift through strategy alone. Because even high-functioning stress is still stress. Even composure can be a form of dysregulation. When your nervous system stays in survival mode, regulation isn't something you achieve; it's something you recover. Not through insight, but through input. Through a different kind of rhythm. One your body has been missing beneath all the systems and structure. You're not failing at regulation.

You've just been trying to manage a biology problem with psychology tools. And your body's not waiting for permission to soften. It's waiting for proof that it's safe.

You Can't Talk a Nervous System into Regulation

You can't reason your way into safety. Because by the time your brain is trying to understand, your body has already made a decision. Regulation doesn't begin with insight. It begins with input. With movement. Rhythm. Pressure. Not words—but signals. The body doesn't need another explanation. It needs to feel—in real time—that it's safe to stop bracing. That it's safe to stay. That's where the rewiring begins.

Movement Isn't Just Output

Most people see movement as output. More reps. More control. More performance. We've been taught: strength equals regulation, fitness equals resilience, endurance equals capacity. But I kept seeing something else. People crushing CrossFit workouts still couldn't slow their breath. High-performers could run marathons but couldn't rest. Their fitness wasn't failing them; it just wasn't what their nervous system was asking for. Because regulation doesn't come from performance. It comes from perception.

People who could hold a plank for two minutes couldn't hold eye contact during conflict. It didn't add up—until I reframed the question: what if movement isn't about performance... but recalibration? Because movement wasn't fixing the pattern. It was the pattern—expressing itself through tremors, tension, and sway. Every micro-movement was the nervous system speaking in its first language: rhythm.

It wasn't asking to be corrected. It was asking to be heard. Movement wasn't the intervention. It was the conversation. And the body needed to lead it.

The First Signs of Something Different

It didn't start as a method. It started as curiosity. What if we took away the pressure? What if movement wasn't a form of control—but an invitation? We began small. Crawling. Cross-body drills. Vestibular resets.

Gentle, rhythmic sequences that mirrored early development. Not to regress—but to rebuild. And things shifted.

A woman who hadn't slept in years dozed off after a rocking drill. A teenage boy, labeled "defiant," sat cross-legged and still after crawling. A therapist—always in control—stopped shaking after rolling on the floor. And one client—barely above a whisper—said: "This is the first time I've felt held... by my own body." These weren't workouts. They were repairs. Signals to the nervous system: you can stop bracing now.

The Costello Method Was Born

Not as a theory. But as a response to what the body was already asking for. What emerged wasn't a formula—it was a three-stage, body-led, brain-supported framework. A method where the body leads, and the brain learns to follow. Not because the body is forced into calm, but because it remembers how to create it. Regulation isn't taught through explanation. It's recalibrated through experience.

When rhythm comes before reflection—when movement comes before mindset—the body softens. And the brain finally receives the signal it's been waiting for.

The Three Phases of the Costello Method

This work isn't linear. It's layered. Each phase meets the body where it is —and builds from there.

PHASE 1: FOUNDATION RESET. We begin with safety. We calm sensory reactivity, integrate primitive reflexes, and rebuild postural stability. This isn't just the warm-up. It's the root system. Before the body can process, perform, or push—it has to feel safe just being. The Foundation Reset teaches the nervous system how to stop defending and start receiving.

PHASE 2 : FORTIFY CONNECTIVITY. Now we build efficiency. We activate the vestibular system, engage the cerebellum, and strengthen sensory-motor coordination. This is where balance begins to replace bracing. By refining how input is processed, the system doesn't have to work so hard to stay upright. Fortify Connectivity helps the nervous system shift from effort to flow.

PHASE 3: FINE-TUNE INTEGRATION. This is where resilience becomes reflex. We layer multi-sequence movement, integrate both hemispheres, and train recovery through transition. Instead of reacting to stress, the system learns to adapt. Fine-Tune Integration restores agility—not by pushing harder, but by moving smarter.

What Makes This Work Different

The Costello Method isn't built on intensity. It's built on input. It doesn't train muscles. It reactivates circuits. It doesn't chase calm. It creates the conditions for it to return. And in this work, safety isn't just the absence of stress—it's the presence of adaptability. The ability: to shift, recover, and return—without collapse or masking. Every drill, every rhythm, every breath serves one purpose—to remind the body that safety isn't something it has to earn—it's something it can return to.

From Output to Orientation

Movement isn't just a way to burn energy. It's how the brain knows where the body is—and whether it's safe to settle. This is why traditional fitness often misses the mark for people stuck in dysregulation. It's not that movement is wrong. It's that the sequence matters. When rhythm, breath, and sensory input lead—the system stops scanning for danger. And in its place rises clarity. Focus. Stability. Trust. Not as a mindset. But as a baseline.

The Invitation

This chapter is a doorway. From performance to pattern. From survival to signal. From forcing calm to following rhythm. You don't have to perform your way into healing. You don't have to earn your way out of dysregulation. You just have to start where your body is—and let it lead the way back. Movement, done with intention, becomes one of the most powerful ways we remember: regulation was never something we had to force. It was something we were always wired to return to.

Pause & Notice

- Have you been "doing the work"—but still feel like your system doesn't shift?
- Do you feel like your body reacts before you even get a vote?
- Have you ever used movement to manage stress, but not to recover from it?
- Do your wellness habits feel like they're helping—or just keeping you afloat?
- Do you ever wonder why you can't feel calm, even when you're doing everything "right"?

You're not missing the tools. Your body might just be missing the sequence.

Key Takeaways

Insight doesn't create regulation. Input does. This chapter marks the shift from understanding your nervous system to working with it—through rhythm, breath, and movement.

Dysregulation isn't always loud. It can look like over-functioning, effort, or trying harder. But regulation doesn't come from performance—it comes from pattern. The Costello Method isn't about intensity. It's about sequencing input the body was always wired to receive.

We don't override the system. We reconnect it—layer by layer, rhythm by rhythm. This isn't about controlling your body. It's about giving your body the signal it's been waiting for: it's safe to stop bracing. You can come back now.

You're not here to manage chaos. You're here to rewire calm, not through effort, but through rhythm. Not by overriding your system, but by rebuilding trust with it—layer by layer. You don't have to chase safety anymore. You can create it. You can come back now.

CHAPTER 9

FOLLOWING THE BODY BACK TO REGULATION

There's a moment I've come to expect. It usually arrives right after someone says: "I've done everything." They've journaled, meditated, cut sugar, and practiced breath work. They've gone to therapy, optimized their routines, and followed every expert. And still, their body feels like it's bracing for impact. Tight chest. Restless sleep. A low-level urgency that won't let go. Not panic. Not collapse. Just that lingering sense that something inside is still holding on.

That's when I remind them: **nothing is broken**. There's just a system that's out of sync. You don't need more tools. You need a new starting point: one that meets your nervous system where it actually lives—in your body.

Why Trying Harder Doesn't Work

Most approaches begin with the brain: change your thoughts, reframe your emotions, manage your behaviors. And when your system is relatively stable, those strategies can help. But most of the people I work with aren't short on insight. They know their patterns. They can name their triggers mid-spiral. They've done the mindset work. The problem isn't awareness. It's access.

By the time they try to regulate, their system is already in motion—breath shortened, muscles braced, heart racing. You can't logic your way out of a state your nervous system hasn't physically exited. **The body leads. The brain follows.** Until we start there, we're speaking the wrong language.

Casey's Pattern: Doing Everything "Right"

Casey was a high-level educator. Insightful, empathic, and deeply committed to growth. She tracked her nervous system like a spreadsheet. Supplements. Somatic therapy. Morning walks. Evening yoga. "I know when I'm dysregulated," she said. "But by the time I reach for a tool... it's too late." She could name the moment her breath changed—but she couldn't stop the spiral. Even her pauses were scheduled.

When we began working together, her movements were clean—but rehearsed. She didn't fidget. She performed calm. And that performance was costing her presence. We started simple. Crawling drills. Rocking. Cross-body movement while listening to a metronome. One day she asked, "Why does this feel more powerful than a 90-minute therapy session?" Her system wasn't resisting insight—it was simply waiting for something it could feel.

What I Started to See in My Clients

It didn't matter if I was working with therapists, athletes, teachers, or high-performing parents. The pattern was the same. They had the tools. They were self-aware. They weren't avoiding the work—they were drowning in it. And when life got loud, their bodies defaulted to defense—despite all the insight.

You're Not Just the Calm—You're the Cue

This was especially true for parents. Especially those parenting kids with big emotions, sensory needs, or neurodivergence. Many of them knew the scripts. They used gentle parenting. They read the books. They paused before reacting. But they couldn't stop the escalation—not because they lacked tools, but because their body was still broadcasting stress.

Children don't regulate because we give them instructions. They regulate because we give them something to mirror. That's co-regulation. Not telling them to calm down, but helping their nervous system borrow your stability until theirs remembers how to return. Your tone. Your posture. Your breath. Your pace. These aren't just signals—they're scaffolding.

If you've ever watched your child spiral despite doing everything "right," it's not a failure. It's feedback. Their system is listening to your system—not your words. That's why in the Costello Framework, we don't just teach the parent to model calm. We help their body become the cue. Not perfection. Just presence their child can attune to.

This Wasn't a Mindset Issue

Or a motivation issue. Their systems had simply never been shown how to feel **safe**. They didn't need more discipline. They needed a **new map**. That map became the **Costello Framework**.

The Costello Framework

A Body-Led, Brain-Supported Model for Real Regulation

This isn't a theory. It's a sequence—based on science, rooted in rhythm, and built to work with how your system actually functions. The Costello Framework doesn't just teach you to cope better. It helps your body *remember* how to recalibrate. You're not just learning a method. You're restoring the rhythm your system was always designed for.

This work unfolds in three phases:

Phase 1: Foundation Reset

Phase 2: Fortify Connectivity

Phase 3: Fine-Tune Integration

Within each phase are practical, body-based inputs that speak the language your nervous system actually understands.

. . .

PHASE 1: FOUNDATION RESET

Stabilize the system. Build safety from the ground up.

- **Step 1:** Identify Nervous System Imbalances

Before a full shutdown or spiral, the body always whispers first. It speaks through tension that never quite dissolves, a breath that tightens just enough to go unnoticed, a mind that struggles to shift gears without friction. Sensitivity to sound, light, and touch isn't weakness—it's communication.

These early signs aren't proof that you're failing; they're messages from a system working overtime to keep you safe, even when no threat is present. In this first step, we begin with noticing. You're not fixing. You're not analyzing. You're simply listening.

Twice a day—once in the morning, once in the evening—pause and scan gently:

- Is my breath full or shallow?
- Are my shoulders lifted or resting?
- Is my gaze darting or still?
- Is my stomach clenched or easy?

Choose one sensation to acknowledge without any agenda to change it. Awareness itself is the beginning of safety. When your body feels heard, it no longer has to shout to get your attention. Regulation doesn't begin by doing more—it begins by noticing earlier.

If you've ever felt like your body was betraying you even after doing everything "right," the truth is simpler and more profound: your body has been speaking to you all along. You're just now learning to understand its language.

- **Step 2:** Calm Sensory Reactivity — Releasing Primitive Reflexes

Some survival patterns are meant to be temporary, designed for infancy and early growth. But when chronic stress, trauma, or missed developmental windows interrupt the process, certain reflexes—like the startle or withdrawal reflex—get stuck running in the background. If you startle easily, flinch at sudden sounds, struggle to relax in stillness, or feel edgy without a clear reason, your system might be caught in an old loop.

In this step, we give the body the developmental experiences it may have missed—not by forcing calm through willpower, but by offering the simple movements that complete those loops naturally. Gentle rocking, crawling patterns, and cross-body motions give your nervous system the sensory input it still craves.

You don't have to force relaxation; you invite it. You've been in protection, not dysfunction. And when you complete these old survival loops, your system stops bracing and starts receiving. It's not that you can't sit still or calm down; it's that your body never felt safe enough to let go. Now, you're giving it a reason to.

- **Step 3:** Rebuild Postural Reflexes

There's a hidden energy cost that comes from holding yourself up when the body's natural support systems aren't firing. You might feel it as shoulders that refuse to soften, a chest that never quite expands, a breath that hovers high and shallow. When postural reflexes are under active, even sitting still feels like work. The body interprets this constant low-grade effort as threat.

In this step, we focus on restoring your innate relationship with gravity. Through gentle developmental sequences—rocking back, rolling forward, rebuilding your center—you invite your body to rediscover what effortless support feels like. When the deep postural muscles reengage automatically, your shoulders drop without you telling them to. Your breath settles into your belly. Calm stops being something you chase, and becomes something you return to, again and again.

The effort you thought was "just how life feels" wasn't inevitable. It was a system waiting to be re-tuned. Safety isn't something you have to create—it's something you remember.

PHASE 2: FORTIFY CONNECTIVITY

Rewire the pathways between regulation and resilience.

- **Step 4:** Activate the Vestibular System

When your body loses its internal sense of orientation—its knowing of where it is in space—everything feels just a little bit more effortful. You might feel dizzy when you move too fast, disconnected while sitting still, or perpetually braced for something to go wrong. The vestibular system, responsible for balance and spatial awareness, plays a silent but powerful role in your sense of safety. When it's under active or overwhelmed, your brain constantly asks: "Where am I?" and "Am I about to fall?"

In this step, we use slow, rhythmic movements—head turns, gentle rolling, balancing on unstable surfaces—to reawaken your body's internal GPS. When your vestibular system recalibrates, your body stops bracing for what it can't quite name. Grounding isn't just a metaphor; it's a physical experience. When your body knows exactly where you are, your mind stops fearing what might happen next.

- **Step 5:** Improve Timing and Transitions

Overwhelm isn't always about how much is happening—it's often about how well your system can move from one thing to the next. When timing circuits in the brain are underdeveloped or overloaded, even simple transitions—like finishing an email and answering a phone call—can feel like slamming on the brakes without warning. The cerebellum, a small but mighty part of your brain, orchestrates smoothness, sequencing, and rhythm across both movement and thought.

In this step, we work on re-timing through patterned, rhythmic activities: marching to a beat, crossing the midline while stepping, coordinating hands and feet. These aren't just exercises; they're recalibration drills for your transitions. As your cerebellum strengthens, you move through physical tasks—and emotional shifts—with more ease. It's not that life got lighter overnight; it's that your system finally learned to dance with it, not brace against it.

- **Step 6:** Balance the Alert + Emotional Systems

When your brain's alert system (Reticular Activating System) and emotional filter (Limbic System) are out of sync, even everyday moments can feel overwhelming. Easily distracted. Sounds seem louder. Tasks feel bigger. Emotions hit harder. Your brain either overreacts to harmless cues or under reacts when real action is needed, keeping you swinging between anxiety and burnout.

In this step, we bring balance back to these two critical systems through bilateral movement, rhythmic breathing, and intentional pacing. These practices synchronize sensory input with emotional regulation, helping your system tune intensity back to reality.

Instead of living in survival mode, you return to a more fluid, responsive state. Regulation isn't about shutting down emotion. It's about restoring proportion. When your internal alarms match the actual size of the challenge, calm stops feeling like a performance—and starts feeling like your default.

PHASE 3: FINE-TUNE INTEGRATION

Build regulation in motion. Make it automatic.

- **Step 7:** Midline Integration

At the heart of adaptability is communication—between the left and right sides of your brain, between the analytical and the intuitive, between thought and action. When that communication is choppy, focus fractures, coordination stutters, and emotional flexibility narrows. You may feel mentally foggy, clumsy, or stuck in repetitive loops of thought or behavior.

Midline integration rebuilds that bridge. Through simple cross-body drills—moving one hand across to the opposite knee, tracing figure-eights in the air, rhythmically reaching across the body—you help your brain hemispheres sync up. This isn't about being faster; it's about being clearer. When your midline pathways strengthen, transitions smooth out. Focus sharpens. Emotional shifts stop feeling like cliffs. You don't think your way to better regulation—you embody it. True resilience isn't just bouncing back; it's staying fluid enough to move between states without getting trapped.

- **Step 8:** Master Multi-Sequence Movement

Life never throws challenges at you one at a time. It weaves complexity into the ordinary—unexpected calls during a busy day, emotional conversations layered over physical exhaustion, multiple sensory demands all at once. To stay grounded when complexity rises, your system needs to practice managing layered inputs without bracing.

In this step, we introduce multi-sequence movement: combining two or three simple tasks at once, adding mild complexity through playful challenge. It could be stepping and clapping to a rhythm, crawling while tapping a pattern, balancing while moving your eyes. These aren't tests —they're rehearsals.

By layering mild complexity under safe, playful conditions, you build agility not just in your muscles, but in your emotions and attention too. Mastery doesn't look like rigidity. It looks like flow—responding to life's curveballs without losing your center.

- **Step 9:** Full Integration in Real Life

Regulation isn't meant to stay in the safe, quiet practice spaces. It's designed to move with you into the messy, beautiful, unpredictable rhythms of real life. Full integration happens when you stop needing to think about regulation—because it's woven into the way you breathe, move, pause, and recover.

In this step, we stop adding complexity and start living the rhythms you've rebuilt. You'll notice it not in grand performances, but in subtle shifts: a deep breath before the meeting, a grounded pause before reacting, a softening in your muscles when stress rises instead of tightening. Calm becomes less of an achievement and more of an anchor. Integration doesn't mean perfection. It means returning, again and again, to the safety and steadiness your body now knows how to find on its own.

This Isn't a Ladder. It's a Loop.

You don't graduate from these steps and never look back. You cycle through them, based on your day, your stress, your needs. Some days you fine-tune. Some days, you crawl. That's not regression. That's regulation.

It's subtle: you breathe deeper—without cue. You pause—without effort. You stop bouncing your leg. You don't shrink when the email arrives. You're still. Not because you're trying—but because your body finally believes it's safe. That's not performance. It's restoration—by design.

Pause & Notice

- Have you done everything "right"—but still feel like your body is bracing?
- Do you notice your breath shortening, your shoulders lifting, your sleep getting lighter—even when your routine is solid?
- Have you ever wondered why your body keeps spiraling, even when your brain knows what's happening?
- Have you turned regulation into another job to manage, instead of a state your body can return to?

This isn't failure. It's feedback. Your system doesn't need more insight. It needs a rhythm it can actually follow.

Key Takeaways

You're not stuck because you haven't tried hard enough. You're stuck because your nervous system is still waiting for a signal it can understand. Most approaches start with the brain. But real regulation starts in the body.

The Costello Framework isn't about effort. It's about **access**. You don't have to push harder to find calm. You don't have to earn your way into regulation.

You just have to start where your body already lives—and give it the sequence it's been waiting for. That's how healing stops being something you perform—and becomes something you return to.

CHAPTER 10

REAL-TIME TOOLS FOR WHEN REGULATION FEELS OUT OF REACH

S am wasn't melting down. He was mid-sentence, typing an email and casually sipping tea during our Zoom session. But something flickered. His voice lost color. His gaze drifted—not unfocused, but untethered. His shoulders were still high, but his presence had quietly slipped out of the frame.

"I'm not sure where I just went," he said, blinking slowly. "I was here— and then I wasn't."

There was no panic. No drama. Just a quiet kind of disconnect—the kind most people don't notice until much later. Not broken. Not unsafe. Just... not fully there.

For people like Sam—and maybe like you—this isn't rare. It's just rarely recognized. We tend to think of nervous system dysregulation as dramatic collapse or emotional chaos. But more often, it looks like this: the slow drift, the hum beneath your skin, the subtle moment you feel "off" but can't explain why. It's the email you reread three times. The conversation you suddenly can't follow. The moment you're going through the motions, but you're not really there.

This chapter doesn't begin with crisis. It begins with those smaller exits. The micro-disconnections. The barely-noticed slippages. The moments that pull you just slightly off center keeping you from returning on your own.

That's where an S.O.S. Reset comes in.

What an S.O.S. Reset Is—and Isn't

An S.O.S. reset stands for System Override Sequence™—though it might as well mean Support on the Spot. It's not a mindset trick or a feel-good hack. It's not about journaling your way to clarity or willing yourself into calm with positive thoughts. It's a short, precise, body-based input that helps your nervous system reorient in real time.

When you're not fully present—but not in full-blown crisis either—these resets act like bridges. They reconnect you to yourself through simple movements that speak in the language your body already understands. No force. No effort. Just a cue your system can recognize and follow.

These don't replace deeper healing—they help you reach it, especially when your system can't on its own.

That's exactly why this chapter matters in the bigger arc of your transformation. Throughout this book, we've been rewiring your nervous system for long-term regulation. But the truth is, life doesn't always wait for a full reset. Sometimes dysregulation sneaks in sideways—at the grocery store, before a meeting, during a bedtime routine, or at 3:00 PM when your brain won't shut off and your body won't catch up. Sometimes all you have are sixty seconds. And sometimes, that's enough.

They're fast, portable, and designed to meet your system in motion. They're not distractions or detours. They're pattern interrupters—micro-movements that deliver a clear message to your body: *You're safe. You're here. You can stop running now.*

What S.O.S. Resets Actually Do

Each S.O.S. Reset is a signal—deliberate, physical, and neurologically precise. These aren't random movements. They're targeted interventions that help your body interrupt the survival loop, reconnect the brain and body, and restore presence and capacity. They don't rely on your ability to focus. They don't require belief. They work because they tap into systems your body already knows how to follow.

Through brainstem activation, resets that use primitive motor patterns —like rolling, marching, or simple cross-body movements—interrupt your body's automatic stress responses: fight, flight, or freeze. Proprioceptive input, like joint compression, deep pressure, or subtle muscle engagement, sends stabilizing signals to your brain. These cues tell your system where you are in space and help you feel grounded again. Vagal tone stimulation—through things like facial movement, or steady breathing—helps shift your body out of high alert and back into the parasympathetic state, where calm, clarity, and flexibility return.

The most powerful part? These systems don't wait for you to calm down before they work. They kick in first—and create the calm that follows.

Movement Isn't Just Movement. It's Message.

Let's pause and reframe something important: not all movement creates regulation. Exercise is valuable—but it doesn't automatically rewire stress. It's easy to confuse motion with healing, especially when you've been told that walking, working out, or "just moving your body" is the best way to feel better. Practices like yoga, Pilates, and strength training absolutely help. They offer rhythm, presence, and structure. But often, the relief they bring fades. Not because they don't work—but because they weren't designed to address the neurological root of dysregulation.

The Costello Method is different. These aren't workouts. They're neurological resets—movement sequences crafted to stimulate under-performing circuits, re-pattern primitive reflexes, and teach your system how to move through the world without bracing. If you've ever felt a flicker of calm after breathwork or a body scan, that wasn't your imagination. That was your nervous system exhaling. What we do here is take that small exhale—and build a roadmap back to it. Again and again. On demand.

Brain Fog Reset: Clear the Clutter, Reclaim Focus

Brain fog isn't laziness. And it's not a lack of motivation. It's a disruption in the communication between the parts of your brain responsible for organizing focus, memory, and clarity. When those internal networks fall out of sync, you feel it. You reread the same sentence three times. You lose track of time. You forget what you were doing—while you're still doing it.

This reset helps restore that internal dialogue. No pushing. No forcing. No trying to "think harder." Just simple, direct inputs that begin to rewire those connections from the ground up—so clarity returns from the inside out.

Brain Fog Reset Routine

- **Shoulder Compression:** Cross your arms and give yourself a hug, squeezing your shoulders. Hold for 10 seconds, then release. Repeat 3 times. Stay grounded and notice the calming effect.

- **Windmills**: Stand tall with feet shoulder-width apart. Twist your torso and reach one hand down toward the opposite foot. Return to center and alternate sides. Do 10 reps per side. Keep your core engaged and your movement controlled.

- **Cheek Puff Breathing**: Inhale slowly through your nose. Puff your cheeks with air, then exhale gently through pursed lips. Repeat for 5 slow cycles. Keep your breath soft and steady.

These movements restore executive function, sharpen focus, and bring your brain back online—without needing willpower to get there.

Anxiety Reset: Calm the System, Regain Control

Anxiety isn't all in your head. It lives in your body—wired into your muscles, your breath, your impulses. It's not just a feeling; it's a full-body state. And when anxiety rises, the goal isn't to outthink it. The goal is to speak to it in the only language it truly understands: sensation, compression, breath, and rhythm. Regulation doesn't come from logic —it comes from contact with the systems that hold the alarm.

Morning Reset: Prime Your System

- **Iron Cross**: Lie on your back with arms out in a "T." Keeping your legs straight, lift one leg and slowly cross it over your body, reaching toward the opposite side. Let your head turn the other way. Pause, then return to center. Do 5 reps per side. Move with control and steady breath.

- **Figure 8's**: Using a pen or your finger, slowly trace a figure 8 in the air or on a surface. Keep your eyes on the movement to engage visual tracking and coordination. Do 10 reps with the right and left hand. Keep your motion smooth and steady.

- **Belly Breathing**: Place a hand on your lower belly. Inhale slowly through your nose, letting your belly rise. Exhale fully through your mouth, feeling your belly fall. Do 4 slow, steady rounds.

When Anxiety Spikes: Regulate Fast

- **Prayer Press**: Bring your palms together at chest height. Press firmly, engaging your arms and shoulders. Hold for 10 seconds, then release. Repeat 5 times. Stay grounded and steady through each round.

- **Cross March**: Bring one knee up to meet the opposite hand. Alternate sides—left hand to right knee, then right hand to left knee. Do 10 reps per side. Keep your core engaged and rhythm steady.

- **Box Breathing**: Inhale for 4 counts. Hold for 4. Exhale for 4. Hold again for 4. Repeat 3–5 times. Keep your breath smooth and even throughout.

In-the-Moment Reset: Discreet and Effective

- **Ankle Rolls**: Lift one foot and rotate your ankle in a slow, circular motion. Do 5 rolls in each direction, then switch sides. Move with control and keep the motion smooth.

- **Palm Press**: Interlace your fingers and press your palms together, squeezing firmly. Hold for 5 seconds, then release. Do 5 reps. Stay steady and grounded through each squeeze.

- **Wrist Flexes**: Extend one arm forward at shoulder height. Flex and extend your wrist—pumping it up and down like a wave. Move smoothly through the full range of motion. Do 5 slow, controlled reps on one side, then switch arms and repeat. Aim for about 5–7 seconds per side.

Whether you're managing anxiety mid-day or preparing for something stressful, this system creates the conditions for calm—before your thoughts catch up.

Mid-Day Brain Booster: Restore Energy and Clarity

Mental fatigue isn't solved by pushing harder. By mid-day, your brain has already reached its capacity. You don't need more discipline. You need a reset. This short routine re-engages your nervous system—gently, quickly, and without requiring focus or overthinking. It's not about doing more. It's about helping your system come back online.

- **Wrist Rolls**: Extend one arm and make slow, controlled circles with your wrist. Do 5 rolls in one direction, then 5 in the other. Repeat on the other side. Keep your fingers relaxed and your motion fluid.

- **Shoulder Shrugs**: Lift both shoulders up toward your ears. Hold for 10 seconds, then release fully. Repeat 5 times. Keep your breath steady and let tension melt on the release.

- **Deep Breaths**: Inhale slowly through your nose. Exhale fully through pursed lips, longer than your inhale. Repeat for 4–6 calming cycles. Let each breath soften your body.

In five minutes or less, this reset shifts you from mental fog to focused presence—no caffeine required.

When to Use These Resets

You don't need a mat. You don't need privacy. You don't even need to believe they'll work. These resets aren't rituals. They're access points— fast, embodied signals that meet you exactly where you are.

Use them between meetings, before a hard conversation, or at the first flicker of "I'm not okay." They take less than a minute. They shift the input—so your system can follow. It doesn't take much. Just one cue. One moment. One interruption in the loop.

What Relief Can Actually Feel Like

Relief doesn't always look like a breakthrough. It doesn't always feel like serenity. Sometimes, it's smaller than that. Quieter. A jaw that softens. A breath that lands. A quiet sense of being here—instead of hovering somewhere outside yourself.

That's what regulation feels like. Not a reward. A return.

Pause & Notice

- Do you find yourself drifting on autopilot through the day?
- Do you snap at small things?
- Do you carry a low hum of urgency, even when nothing's wrong?

You don't need to override your nervous system. You don't need a strategy or a script. You just need one cue your body recognizes—and is willing to follow home.

Key Takeaways

Regulation doesn't always start with a breakthrough. Sometimes, it starts with a breath. A march. A flicker of presence returning to your chest. These S.O.S. Resets aren't workarounds. They're doorways—simple, precise signals that bring you back when everything else feels too far away.

No focus required. No permission needed. Just one clear moment that reminds your system: you're not spiraling. You're landing.

Scan the QR code below to access additional information on resets and movement practices.

•••

PART III

WHEN THE BODY FALLS OUT OF SYNC

Sometimes, even when you know the tools... your body doesn't budge. You've tracked your triggers. Built awareness. Stayed consistent with your practice. But the spiral still comes. The shutdown still hits. And the calm you've been working so hard for still feels just out of reach.

This part of the book is for those moments. For the ones who say, "I've done everything—but I still feel off." For the people who can name their pattern in real time—but still can't stop it from happening. For the nervous systems that don't look dysregulated from the outside, but are bracing silently, every single day.

Now that you understand the method, it's time to uncover what your body has been trying to say all along. These chapters reveal the physical underpinnings of mental and emotional symptoms—from balance and coordination to focus, energy, and emotional steadiness.

This is where the deeper work begins. Here, we explore the invisible barriers that keep the system stuck. Despite all your effort.

Retained reflexes that hijack your calm before you can reach it. Sensory mismatches that flood your system, even in quiet moments. Postural gaps that leave your body holding tension it was never meant to carry.

These aren't flaws. They're not failures. They're signals—asking to be decoded, not dismissed.

Because what looks like "too sensitive" or "too reactive" on the surface... might actually be a body working overtime just to stay upright.

This part isn't about fixing. It's about finally listening. And when you stop fighting your symptoms—and start following their lead—that's when the real rewiring begins.

CHAPTER 11

SENSORY REACTIVITY, WHEN THE WORLD LANDS TOO LOUD

You wouldn't have called Sophia dysregulated—not at first. She was composed. Thoughtful. A little quiet. She didn't melt down. She didn't panic. She didn't lash out.

The moment she walked in, I could feel the tension—her body already bracing before anything happened. Her eyes flicked up to the lights before she found my face. Her hands stayed tucked inside her sleeves. Her shoulders barely moved, but every flicker of light or sound made her pull back—just a little."

She wasn't shutting down. She was bracing. Not against a crisis. But against the everyday. Too bright. Too loud. Too much. When I asked her how long it had felt this way, she said: "I don't know. I think I've always just... managed. But it's exhausting."

The Hidden Cost of a Reactive System

Sophia wasn't "too sensitive." Her system was too exposed. By mid-morning, she'd already started dimming the world. Fluorescent lights triggered headaches. Background conversations made her lose her train of thought. Certain fabrics made her want to crawl out of her skin.

And it's not always about sensitivity. Sometimes the system under-responds instead—missing social cues, zoning out, or not hearing your name the first three times. Dysregulation lives at both ends of the sensory spectrum: hyper- and hypo-reactivity.

This wasn't about preference or attitude; it was survival. Because sensory reactivity doesn't start in the mind. It starts in the body's filtering systems: the systems that interpret light, sound, motion, and touch to decide what's safe—or what's not. When those systems misfire, everything becomes signal. And signal becomes threat.

It Doesn't Always Look Like Overwhelm

Sensory overload doesn't always look like a meltdown. Sometimes it looks like silence. Sometimes it looks like disappearing in plain sight.

The person who cancels plans without knowing why. The one who zones out mid-conversation—not because they're bored, but because for them, the noise is louder than your words. The person who smiles, nods, keeps it together—while their nervous system is screaming under the surface.

Sophia didn't shut down. She adapted. Soft clothes. Predictable spaces. Guarded expression. She called it "preserving energy." But really—she was spending all of it, every minute, just trying to stay regulated in a system that never learned how.

What Was Actually Happening

Sophia wasn't fragile. She wasn't broken. She'd been carrying a nervous system that was never taught how to filter the world. Every flicker of light. Every shifting sound. Every motion at the edge of her vision, and her brain registered it all.

Without the right developmental wiring, and without a baseline of safety, her system defaulted to vigilance. And what we found, underneath all the bracing, was something few adults are told to look for: primitive reflexes that had never fully integrated.

The Reflexes That Resurface

These early movement patterns—like the Moro reflex (startle) or the Tonic Labyrinthine Reflex (postural)—are meant to help infants survive. They should fade as the nervous system matures.

But under chronic stress, trauma, or skipped developmental stages... they don't. They linger. Or they re-emerge later in life. And when they do, the world lands harder. Louder. Sharper.

Because your system isn't responding like an adult. It's defending like an infant. Sophia wasn't overreacting, her body was running an outdated operating system that said: everything is a threat until proven otherwise.

How We Rewired the System

Proprioception: The Body's Internal GPS

Her brain didn't trust where she was in space—so it scanned. Constantly. We introduced deep pressure, joint compression, and slow, sustained isometric holds. The message was simple: You're here. You're safe. You don't need to brace.

Vestibular Activation: Teaching the Brain to Track Motion Calmly

Gentle rocking. Directional head turns. Eyes fixed on a stable target. Her dizziness faded. Her posture softened. She began to move—not to escape—but to settle.

Reflex Integration: Clearing the Noise of Primitive Defenses

Sophia's system was still running protective reflexes that belonged to a younger, more fragile stage of development. We moved through them slowly. Repetitively. Her body began to reorganize—not through thought, but through rhythm. Not through control, but through memory.

Where We Left Off with Sophia

Sophia didn't leave with a list of hacks. She left with access. She walked into my office one morning and paused before she sat down.

"I used to get a headache the minute I walked into this room," she said. "I didn't even notice the light today."

Not because she toughened up. Because her body no longer needed to fight. She still has days when the world feels sharp. But now, she knows what her system is doing—and what it needs to come back.

What This Means for You

If you find yourself shrinking from noise, light, or crowds—not because you're afraid, but because it all just feels like too much... You're not fragile. You're not failing. You may just be filtering input with a system that was never shown how.

A system still running defenses that were supposed to fade—but never did. Sensory reactivity isn't a personality flaw. It's a nervous system calling for clarity. And when you begin to train that system with the inputs it missed? Calm stops being something you perform. It becomes something your body knows how to return to.

———

Pause & Notice

- Have you ever avoided a place—not because you were anxious, but because the stimulation felt impossible to manage?
- Do certain textures, sounds, or environments make you flinch —or brace—without knowing why?
- Have you ever left a conversation and realized you missed it entirely—because your body was still tracking everything else?

Those aren't quirks. They're clues—signals from a system asking for support, not scrutiny. And when you start to listen, everything begins to shift.

Key Takeaways

Dysregulation doesn't always scream. Sometimes it whispers—through the body of someone who looks composed, but never fully lands. If you flinch at loud sounds, avoid bright spaces, or feel drained by normal days, your system may not be overreacting. It may be over-processing.

When the nervous system misses key developmental steps or stays stuck in primitive reflexes, the world doesn't just feel overwhelming—it feels unsafe. Not because you're fragile, but because your system never learned how to filter. Sophia didn't need to toughen up. She needed to retrain her body's baseline. With the right combination of pressure, rhythm, and vestibular calm, her system stopped scanning and began to settle.

That's the shift this chapter offers: from bracing to receiving. From filtering everything to finding ease again. Calm doesn't come from over-riding your sensitivity. It comes from giving your nervous system the clarity it's been missing.

CHAPTER 12

BODY CONTROL, WHEN STRENGTH ISN'T ENOUGH

You can often tell by how someone stands. Not anxious. Not anxious. Not unraveling. Just bracing—shifting weight from foot to foot. Breath held just high enough to stay upright. Knees locked with a tension they don't even notice. Not because they're stressed out, but because their system is doing what reflexes should have done.

I see it every day—in therapists and executives, athletes and parents. Their posture says power, but underneath, their body is whispering, "I'm managing." And managing—quietly, constantly—is its own kind of exhaustion.

When Movement Is Manual

Burt was sharp. Warm. Measured. Mid-40s. Worked in tech. Kept spreadsheets for everything from workouts to meals. Wore a smart ring. Tracked his REM cycles. Had a breath work app and used it.

But when he walked into my space, his body was already talking. "I lift. I stretch. I'm strong," he said. "But I never feel settled." He smiled like it was a joke. It wasn't. I could feel the vulnerability behind that grin.

He stood slightly off-center, his feet unsure where to land. His fingers twitched when he tried to relax. And before we even got into our first drill, he let out a long sigh and said: "I didn't realize how much I was holding."

That was the moment I knew. This wasn't about strength. This was about a system that had never learned how to let go. Most people think body control is about strength. Muscle tone. Core work. Physical capability. But that's not it. True body control is what you don't have to think about. It's the way your spine aligns when you walk across a room. The way your head balances without bracing your jaw. The way you sit without slouching or stiffening.

It's movement that feels like presence, not performance. When your nervous system is wired for control, movement flows. When it's not? Even strong bodies compensate. They hold. They grip. They burn through energy trying to stay vertical.

That was Burt. Not resisting rest—just never able to arrive in it.

What His System Was Missing

It wasn't willpower. It wasn't fitness. It was wiring.

We think of posture as a strength issue. But it's a reflex issue—an internal GPS built through developmental patterns. The nervous system relies on reflexes to automate posture and balance: Righting Reflexes to align the head and spine. Equilibrium Reflexes to recover from shifts in movement. Tonic Neck Reflexes to coordinate the head, limbs, and core in motion.

When these reflexes integrate in childhood, posture becomes automatic. But when they don't—or when early stress, injury, or trauma delays that development—they don't just disappear. They linger. Or they resurface.

In adulthood, these retained reflexes show up as micro-compensations: Tight shoulders even when you're relaxed. Locked knees during conversations. A jaw that grips the minute stillness hits. Your body does what those missing reflexes should have done. And that costs energy—quietly, constantly.

When Strength Stops Working

"I can deadlift 200 pounds," Burt told me. "But I trip over sidewalk cracks." That was the clue. Not a fitness gap, but a communication lag.

His strength was high. But his coordination was improvised. He was holding his body together through tension—not trust. When this pattern shows up, it often looks like: Strength without steadiness. Flexibility without resilience. Endurance paired with subtle, chronic fatigue. These aren't personality quirks. They're survival strategies. They're what happens when reflexes stay unfinished: the body tries to fill in the gaps.

Rewiring from the Ground Up

We didn't start with workouts. We started with recalibration. Simple, quiet drills that restored reflexive communication between brain and body.

Rocking drills to rebuild midline orientation. Crawling patterns to reintroduce cross-body coordination. Standing shifts to reawaken subtle balance mechanisms. Breath-driven core work to allow support without strain.

At first, Burt resisted. "I'm used to pushing myself," he said. "This feels too easy." But a few weeks in, everything shifted. His knees stopped locking. His breath dropped deeper—without effort. He could stand still ... without thinking about it. Not because he worked harder. But because his system stopped trying to survive gravity.

Inputs That Restore Automatic Control

We weren't building muscle; we were rebuilding communication. The missing signals were simple but powerful: joint compression to ground his body in space. Vestibular input to recalibrate his internal balance. Reflex drills to complete developmental sequences left behind decades ago. Proprioceptive feedback to anchor him back into his own structure.

This wasn't about perfect posture. It was about reclaiming ease. And slowly, Burt stopped moving like he was bracing for impact. He started moving like someone who trusted his body to hold him.

This Work Isn't About Fitness

It's for the ones who say: "I'm always tense—even when I'm resting." "Stillness takes more energy than motion." "My body's strong, but it doesn't feel steady."

These aren't red flags of motivation. They're signs of compensation. They mean your system is asking for support—and trying to hold itself together without the wiring it needs.

You don't need to get stronger. You need to get connected. And when we offer that connection, the system softens. Not because it's being disciplined—but because it's being heard.

Where We Left Off with Burt

It didn't end in a breakthrough. It ended in a moment so subtle, it almost went unnoticed. One afternoon after a session, he paused at the door and said: "I walked across the parking lot today, and I didn't think about my posture. I just... walked." That was it. Not because he was performing. But because, for the first time, his body was moving with him—not in spite of him.

Pause & Notice

- Do you feel like your body is strong—but never truly at ease?
- Does stillness feel more like a challenge than a relief?
- Do you catch yourself shifting, fidgeting, or bracing—even in quiet moments?
- What if that tension isn't a habit... but a survival strategy?
- What if your body isn't resisting stillness—but surviving it?

This doesn't change through force or control. It changes through re-integration, when your body finally remembers how to let go.

Key Takeaways

Strength without stability isn't regulation—it's compensation. If you feel tense even at rest, if stillness takes more effort than motion, or if your posture requires constant management, your body may be filling in for reflexes that never fully wired.

Retained reflexes don't mean you're weak. They mean your nervous system is still working around missing pieces—burning energy to stay upright instead of moving with ease. Burt didn't need to get stronger. He needed to stop bracing. And when we fed his system the inputs it missed—rocking, cross-patterning, joint compression—his body stopped managing posture and started embodying it.

This isn't about fixing your form. It's about restoring the reflexes that make ease possible. Because regulation isn't how well you hold yourself together. It's how freely your body holds you.

CHAPTER 13

SPATIAL AWARENESS, WHEN MOVEMENT DOESN'T LAND

I knew something was off before Ethan even sat down. He seemed calm, but something was off. He wasn't visibly overwhelmed. But his movements told a quieter story, one I've learned to recognize. His eyes flicked briefly to the overhead light, his body veering half a degree off-center as he reached for the chair. Not hesitating. Just adjusting.

His posture was upright, even confident. But every step looked like it required just a little too much attention. Like he was moving through water instead of air. Ethan wasn't clumsy. He was compensating. Not in big, dramatic ways, but in the subtle, background ways that reveal a deeper truth: his nervous system was managing motion, rather than inhabiting it. And that kind of control? It comes at a cost.

When You're Moving—but Not Quite Landing

Ethan was sharp, thoughtful, and self-aware. He came in with a question, not a complaint: "Why does movement feel like work when it shouldn't?" He described what many clients never find the words for: the quiet sense of being a step behind his body. Not out of sync exactly —but always adjusting. Always tracking.

He noticed it in everyday moments: missing a stair step by half an inch. Overshooting when reaching for a door. Turning too quickly and feeling momentarily displaced. "It's like I'm never quite... inside my own motion," he said. His nervous system was doing the job of orientation manually. That's the hidden layer most people miss. It's not about being uncoordinated. It's about the body second-guessing its own location in space—and the brain trying to fill in the gaps.

What Spatial Disconnection Really Feels Like

When your spatial awareness is dialed in, you don't notice it. You reach, turn, shift, and walk without thinking. Your body knows where it is—and your brain doesn't have to check. But when that awareness is disrupted, even basic movement becomes effortful.

You start to manage your motion like a to-do list: grip here, adjust there, hold just so. It doesn't look like distress. It looks like constant control. For Ethan, it showed up as micromanagement. Not of his schedule—but of his physical experience. And no amount of strength or stretching was helping him feel more grounded. Because what he needed wasn't output. It was orientation.

The Quiet History Behind Disconnection

As we dug deeper, the patterns began to emerge. He never crawled as a baby—just went straight to walking. He had frequent ear infections in early childhood. He hated gymnastics as a kid—not because of effort, but because he always felt like the room was spinning. None of it had registered as meaningful at the time. But the nervous system remembered.

His brain had never fully developed a reliable map of where he was in space. So it had spent decades scanning—adjusting, compensating, and bracing. Just to stay upright. And like so many others, he thought the issue was effort. He'd tried harder, worked out more, focused better. But you can't will your way into spatial awareness. You have to rebuild the signals underneath.

How We Helped His Body Land Again

We didn't overhaul his routine. We didn't "train balance." We restored feedback. We started with small things: joint compression to anchor proprioception, vestibular drills like rocking and gentle head turns to re-engage orientation, cross-patterned crawling to synchronize hemi-spheres, reflex integration to clear out noise his system didn't even know it was carrying.

At first, it felt almost too simple. "This is like toddler *P.E.* (physical educations)," he joked, half amused, half doubtful. The movements were slow, controlled—almost childlike in their simplicity. But he kept going.

By the end of the first week, subtle shifts began to surface. His breath dropped lower into his belly. His steps grew quieter, more fluid. He could pivot without bracing or overcorrecting. Then one day, while describing a walk to the coffee shop, he paused. A moment passed. "I didn't think about how I was walking," he said quietly. "I just... walked. No tension. No second-guessing. My body just knew what to do." That was the moment. Not because it was dramatic. But because it was different. His system wasn't managing his movement anymore. It was moving —with him.

This Is What You Might Be Missing

If you've ever said: "I bump into things all the time." "I always feel just slightly off." "I can't tell if I'm tense until I stop." You're not imagining it. Your body might be doing its best to move without a clear map.

This isn't about attention. It's not about grace. It's about recalibration. And when we give the nervous system the signals it's been missing—signals of position, rhythm, and orientation—something changes. You stop adjusting. You start arriving. Movement becomes less about managing and more about trust.

Where We Left Off with Ethan

Some days, the world still moved too fast. But his system no longer defaulted to scan-and-correct mode. He didn't have to sit down and brace. He didn't fidget through the session. He didn't double-check the path on his way out. He stood. He moved. He left the room with presence—not just posture. That's what regulation in motion looks like.

Not perfection. But permission. To be in your body—without holding it all together.

Pause & Notice

- Have you ever felt slightly off in your own movement, like you're managing your steps instead of simply taking them?
- Do you find yourself bracing, even in calm moments, or needing to "think" about how you move through a room?
- Does tension only reveal itself once you pause?

These aren't quirks. They're nervous system cues asking to be recalibrated. You don't need to be more mindful—you need your body to feel safer inside its own motion.

Key Takeaways

Disconnection doesn't always feel dramatic. Sometimes it feels like managing movement in slow motion. Like being half a step behind your own body. Like tracking every motion just to feel okay. When spatial systems like the vestibular and proprioceptive circuits are underdeveloped or overwhelmed, the body compensates—quietly, constantly. Not because you're clumsy, but because your nervous system is doing the job reflexes should have done.

That kind of micromanagement doesn't show up as breakdown—it shows up as effort. Bracing. Overcorrection. And the fatigue that follows. Ethan didn't need better posture. He needed feedback. With the right inputs—rocking, crawling, orientation drills—his system began to trust itself.

His body stopped asking permission to move. And slowly, movement became something he didn't have to think about. It just flowed. That's what regulation in motion really means—not perfection, but the quiet knowing: "I'm safe in my own steps."

CHAPTER 14

PROCESSING SPEED, WHEN YOU'RE JUST A BEAT BEHIND

I knew something was off the moment Jordan started speaking—not because he stumbled or was unclear, but because I could see it in his eyes: the thought was there, but the words were lagging behind.

He paused mid-sentence, furrowed his brow, then said with a half-laugh, "It's like my mouth can't keep up with my brain."

He wasn't panicked or confused, but the delay was real. Jordan wasn't lost in thought. He was caught in the space between knowing and delivering.

And in that space, the same frustration I've heard from dozens of clients started to surface: "I'm not slow. But I feel behind." "I know what I want to say—I just can't say it fast enough." "I leave conversations thinking, 'Why couldn't I just respond in time?'"

Jordan wasn't missing insight. His system was missing speed. And that's not a mindset issue. It's a nervous system pattern, one that can be rewired through the body.

When Timing Doesn't Match Capacity

At first, I assumed it was anxiety. Or maybe attention overload. But the more stories I heard, the clearer the pattern became:

These weren't clients in distress. They were present. Capable. Highly self-aware. But something about the timing of their response didn't land.

It showed up in small, persistent ways: Pausing mid-sentence—not from doubt, but from lag. Getting lost in thought during fast-paced meetings. Feeling like your ideas are sharp but your delivery stumbles. Needing more time to "ramp up" than others. They weren't slow thinkers. They were navigating a system that couldn't move fast enough—yet.

What Processing Speed Really Means

We tend to think of processing speed as a cognitive issue—how quickly you think, decide, or speak. But in practice, processing speed is deeply embodied.

It's the smoothness of the input-to-output loop: Your body receives information → Your brain interprets it → Your system responds in real time.

And when there's friction in that loop, everything feels... a half-step behind. Even if your ideas are crystal clear.

That friction can come from anywhere: Reflexes that never fully integrated. A vestibular system that struggles to track motion. Postural tone that's too tense or too loose. Sensory noise that floods the system.

And the result? A delay—not in your intelligence, but in your delivery.

What I Saw in Jordan

Jordan was brilliant. A strategist. A team leader. He didn't struggle with ideas. He struggled with timing. "I feel like I buffer," he told me. "Like I'm running on a slower frequency than the room I'm in."

He'd trained his mind. He'd practiced mindfulness. He'd rehearsed scripts before meetings and social events. But none of it changed the delay. Because the delay wasn't in his mind. It was in the circuitry between mind and motion. So instead of giving him more cognitive tools, we gave his nervous system the one thing it hadn't had: a new rhythm.

Rebuilding the Timing Loop

We didn't push him to respond faster. Instead, we slowed his system down enough to rebuild trust in movement—then layered in speed.

That began with cross-body drills to sync hemispheres, gaze stabilization to reduce overload, and breath work to integrate rhythm and timing.

Movement wasn't used to stimulate output, but to clarify the path. And as his system found that rhythm, the delay shortened. Not because he tried harder. Because his body started moving with his thoughts.

Where We Left Off with Jordan

It wasn't a dramatic transformation. But it was unmistakable. Jordan came in one day and said, "I sat in a meeting, shared an idea, and didn't second-guess myself. I didn't replay the moment later. I just... spoke. And it landed." That's when I knew: His nervous system had stopped trying to catch up. It had arrived.

What This Means for You

If you've ever felt like your thoughts are sharp, but your delivery is scattered... if you leave conversations wondering why the words didn't come faster... if you know what to say but freeze in the space between...

Please hear this: You're not slow or falling behind. You're protecting. You're just moving on a circuit that needs a little rewiring. And when your body finds its rhythm, your brain won't need to push anymore. It will just... respond.

Pause & Notice

- Do you ever buffer before responding—not from doubt, but delay?
- Do you fumble for words you know you have?
- Do you feel mentally clear but physically slow?

This isn't about thinking faster. It's about helping your body catch the rhythm your mind is already moving in—because that kind of clarity begins in the body.

Key Takeaways

Processing speed isn't just about how fast you think—it's about how well your system moves information from body to brain and back again. When there's friction in that loop, even the clearest thoughts can feel trapped behind a wall of delay. That's not dysfunction. It's a nervous system out of sync with its own timing.

Jordan didn't need to push his brain harder. He needed his body to catch the rhythm. Through movement, rhythm, and sensory feedback, his system stopped buffering and started responding. He didn't speak faster because he tried harder. He spoke more clearly because his nervous system finally felt safe enough to respond in real time.

That's the shift this chapter offers: from pressure to perform, to permission to arrive. Because when your body moves in sync with your thoughts, clarity isn't something you chase—it's something you meet.

CHAPTER 15

THE REGULATION ENGINE

I t's always the high-functioners. They come in sharp and self-aware. On paper, they're doing everything right—cutting sugar, meditating, breath work, sleep hygiene, journaling, infrared saunas. The works. But under the surface? Their systems are buzzing.

I've sat across from people who looked like they had it together. They were articulate. Reflective. Attentive. They spoke calmly—even about stress. They described their experiences with precision. But their breath never reached their ribs. Their shoulders stayed high, their voice a beat too tight, their eyes tracking just a little too fast.

One client, Jamie, said it like this: "I'm tired, but I can't land. I'm either pushing or crashing. Even rest doesn't feel restful." Her system wasn't shutting down. It just couldn't downshift. And that's what most people miss: regulation isn't about staying calm all the time. It's about knowing how to move between states—and when that gear shift breaks down, everything gets harder. You don't burn out from intensity alone. You burn out when your system forgets how to recover.

The Hidden Dial Behind Focus, Energy, and Emotion

I call it the *Regulation Engine*—the part of your nervous system responsible for switching states smoothly. It decides how you recover from stress, how long you can sustain attention, and how you emotionally respond to the world around you.

When it's working, you move through life like a well-tuned machine: You stay alert without being anxious. You rest without crashing. You focus without force. But when it's out of sync? Small tasks feel uphill. Emotions feel disproportionate. You feel either overstimulated or flat-lined—and never quite right.

Jamie wasn't lazy. She wasn't unaware. She was wired in a way that made calm feel out of reach. She had insight. But she didn't have access.

What the Regulation Engine Actually Is

Beneath the language of emotion and thought are two major players shaping your daily experience:

1. The Reticular Activating System (RAS):

Your brain's internal spotlight. It filters sensory input and determines what's worth your attention. When it's working well, you can stay focused, adapt to new environments, and stay balanced in your energy. When it's off, you either absorb everything—or nothing lands.

2. The Limbic System:

Your emotional processor and alarm system. It decides how you react to internal and external cues. When dysregulated, it amplifies small stressors or mutes big ones—leaving you reactive or numb, and unsure why.

Together, these two systems create the dial for your internal state. I call that dial your Regulation Engine.

Dysregulation Doesn't Always Look Loud

Sometimes it's subtle: Restlessness that makes stillness uncomfortable. Irritability that hits before you even register frustration. Mental fatigue that feels like trying to think through fog. Tears that show up in quiet moments—without any clear reason. Sleep that doesn't restore.

· · ·

I've seen clients who can lead teams, host workshops, and run households—only to collapse the moment they're alone. Not because they're weak. Because their system never learned how to return to baseline.

Jamie's Performance Mask

Jamie was a leader. A teacher. A mom. The kind of person others came to for support. She'd done therapy, practiced mindfulness, tracked her HRV. She was doing everything the wellness world said would help.

But she was exhausted. Not from doing too much—but from never feeling done. "I can't stop," she told me. "When I try, I feel worse. So I keep going." Her nervous system wasn't resisting rest. It had forgotten how to receive it. We weren't dealing with mindset. We were dealing with a wiring issue.

Why the Old Tools Stop Working

Most emotional regulation tools rely on a system that's already online: Positive affirmations. Reframing. Box breathing. Meditation. Gratitude lists. They can help. But only if your system is already available to receive them.

If your RAS is over activated or your limbic system is signaling threat, those tools land too late. You can't meditate your way out of a system that's already spiraling. You can't talk yourself into regulation if your breath is locked and your body is bracing.

The tools aren't wrong. They're just mistimed. And when the Regulation Engine is offline, you can't fix the system from the top down. You have to go through the body.

Relief Isn't Rewiring

This is where a lot of well-meaning guidance leads people astray. Because yes—breath work can help. So can yoga, Pilates, long walks, or a good sweat. But here's the key: just because something feels better in the moment doesn't mean it's rewiring your stress response.

Relief and regulation aren't the same thing.

What makes the Costello Method different isn't that it uses movement —it's that it sequences movement to restore specific neurological functions. We're not just trying to relax. We're retraining reflexes. Reintegrating the body's early blueprints. Teaching your nervous system how to shift states smoothly again—not once, but on demand.

Your existing practices may contain elements of rhythm, breath, and balance. That's why they feel good. But this method is something else entirely. It's not a wellness routine. It's a neurological restoration process. And when done with intention, it doesn't just calm you—it gives your system back its capacity to recover.

If you've been working out, stretching, meditating—and still burning out—it's not because you're doing it wrong. It's because your system doesn't need more effort. It needs the right kind of input.

Rebuilding the Regulation Engine

The nervous system is adaptable. It learns from input. When we rewire it through movement, rhythm, breath, and coordination, we're not just calming down. We're teaching the system how to shift states safely—on demand.

Phase 1: Reset – Teach the System How to Let Go

The first thing Jamie needed wasn't discipline. It was permission to exhale.

We used: ground-based movement to signal safety. Weighted pressure and tactile input to calm hypervigilance. Breath-led drills that helped the body release without collapsing.

Her feedback? "This is the first time I've felt still—without feeling frozen." Her system wasn't resisting rest. It just hadn't known how to access it.

Phase 2: Strengthen – Make Regulation Repeatable

Once her system remembered calm, we built stability around it.

We added: visual tracking drills to engage the RAS without flooding it.

Midline sequencing to reintroduce timing and coordination. Vestibular resets that taught her system to tolerate motion and transition.

Her sleep got deeper. Her emotional recovery got faster. Conflict didn't spiral her. Rest didn't feel threatening. She wasn't working harder. She was processing cleaner.

Phase 3: Integrate – Return to Real Life with Resilience

This is where regulation becomes more than a practice. It becomes part of who you are.

We simulated stress—lightly: timed transitions between tasks. Movement drills with layered input. Coordinated challenges that tested her ability to shift, recover, and return.

Jamie didn't need a system that made her calm all the time. She needed one that could come back to calm—automatically. And that's exactly what began to happen.

You Don't Have to Earn Calm

Here's what I want you to hear: regulation isn't a reward for effort. It's a function of design. Your system was built to flex, adapt, and stabilize. If that's not happening, it doesn't mean you're broken. It means your inputs need to change.

The Regulation Engine isn't something you force into gear. It's something you train—through rhythm, breath, coordination, and feedback. When those come online, your system remembers how to return. Not with force. With familiarity.

Where We Left Off with Jamie

She still had hard days. But something shifted. She texted me one afternoon: "My daughter spilled smoothie all over the kitchen floor. I was about to yell. Then I noticed—I was holding my breath. I exhaled. And I just cleaned it up. No spiral. No shame. Just... handled."

That's the work. Not perfect. Not performance. Just presence—on purpose.

Pause & Notice

- Where does your system go under pressure?
- Do you ramp up—or shut down?
- Do you brace—even when nothing's wrong?
- Does rest feel like a chore instead of a gift?

These aren't quirks. They're signals. And when you start giving your nervous system what it actually needs to shift—everything else gets easier. You don't have to chase regulation. You just have to train your system to return to it. And that's what this next part of the journey is all about.

Key Takeaways

Regulation isn't about staying calm—it's about knowing how to shift. When the nervous system forgets how to downshift, rest stops feeling restful. Focus starts taking force. And recovery becomes another thing you can't quite reach. Jamie wasn't burned out because she was weak. She was burned out because her system never got to stop.

Most tools rely on a body that's already online. But when the Regulation Engine—your internal dial for alertness, rest, and resilience—is offline, you can't think your way back to balance. You have to retrain it through rhythm, movement, breath, and feedback. That's how the system learns to shift again—without bracing, spiraling, or crashing.

Jamie didn't need to get calmer. She needed her body to feel safe moving between states. And once it did, regulation stopped being something she performed—and became something she could return to. That's not a mindset shift. That's nervous system restoration.

CHAPTER 16

MIDLINE SYNCHRONIZATION

Y ou can usually tell before they speak. Not from what they say—
but from how they move. A glance that doesn't quite land. A
stride that overshoots the corner just slightly. The way they fumble for a
water bottle and knock it—just a little—off target.

They're not panicked. They're not shut down. They're just... off. And if
you ask them, they might not even know how to describe it.

But I've heard the same line a dozen ways: "I'm not clumsy, but I'm not
smooth either." "I feel like I'm always one step behind—physically or
mentally." "I know what I want to do, but my body doesn't always
cooperate."

This isn't a personality trait. It's a coordination issue. And more often
than not, the root of that disconnection lives in something few people
ever consider: midline synchronization.

The Bridge You Didn't Know Was Missing

Your midline is the invisible line that divides your body—and your brain
—in half. One hemisphere controls the opposite side of your body.
Every time you read, reach, write, shift, or respond—you're asking those
two sides to coordinate.

When that communication flows well, things work: You move fluidly. You read without losing your place. You shift tasks without resistance. You feel connected—inside and out.

But when that bridge is glitchy? Even sharp, regulated people can feel foggy, disjointed, or off-balance. And because the signs are subtle, most people don't recognize what's happening.

What It Looks Like in Real Life

Midline issues don't show up as chaos. They show up as friction. Tiny moments of disconnection. You bump into doorframes more than most. You zone out during conversations—not from disinterest, but from fatigue. You drop things. You lose your place mid-sentence.

You hate multitasking, not because it's hard, but because the shifts are jarring. It's not about effort. It's about inefficiency. Your system is doing its best without clear signals. And when that happens, the brain has to micromanage what the body should already know how to do.

It's not laziness. It's lag.

What Was Happening in the Room

I remember Jill—a 37-year-old graphic designer who came in with what she called "a weird kind of brain fog." "I can focus, but it takes more energy than it should," she said. "My body doesn't feel clumsy, exactly... it just doesn't feel like mine."

She had great posture. Clear articulation. A calm demeanor. But she'd pause every few seconds to shift in her seat, like her body was trying to find alignment but couldn't. We ran a simple drill: a cross-body reach with coordinated eye movement. Her rhythm was delayed. Her gaze lagged. Her arms stiffened.

"That felt weird," she said. "Like my body didn't know how to get from one side to the other."

That moment wasn't a test. It was a mirror. Her system hadn't built—or had lost—some of the neural bridges that allow movement and attention to work together. And until we restored that communication, she'd keep burning energy just to stay present.

What Midline Synchronization Actually Is

Midline synchronization is what lets your body and brain coordinate efficiently. At the neurological level, it relies on two major systems:

1. The Corpus Callosum – the bridge between your left and right brain hemispheres. It transfers information so your body can act as a unified whole.

2. The Cerebellum – your brain's rhythm and timing center. It refines movement, sequencing, and fluidity.

When either of these systems underperform, the result isn't chaos—it's effort. You're always adjusting. Re-centering. Re-focusing. Even when it doesn't look like it on the outside.

The Subtle Cost of Disconnection

If you've ever said things like: "I can't track my thoughts and actions at the same time." "I'm not coordinated but I'm not sure why." "Transitions throw me off more than they should." "I drop things even though I'm paying attention"... it might not be about attention. It might be about connection.

Because when your body's communication is lagging, your brain has to pick up the slack. And that extra effort? It doesn't just burn energy. It eats focus, timing, and flow.

You're not uncoordinated. You're un-integrated.

Rebuilding Midline Synchronization

This isn't about training harder. It's about retraining smarter—through rhythm, repetition, and intentional input.

Phase 1: Reset – Reestablish the Map

We begin by anchoring left and right in the sensory system. Ground-based cross-pattern movements like crawling and rolling. Rhythmic vestibular input: rocking, swinging, shifting weight. Breath and compression drills to reduce static in the sensory field. Clients often describe this as "finding their center" again.

Phase 2: Strengthen – Build the Bridge

Next, we train the system to cross, communicate, and sequence. Cross-lateral drills (e.g., elbow-to-knee tapping, marching, contralateral reaches). Visual tracking across midline. Coordination patterns layered with rhythm and breath.

This is where things start to click. People move with less effort. Read with more focus. Transition without tension. They say: "I didn't lose my place." "I finally feel organized—in my body."

Phase 3: Optimize – Make it Automatic

Now we take those patterns into real-world stressors. Dual-tasking drills (e.g., movement + recall, breath + balance). Midline reversals (switching lead side in a movement sequence). Breath-to-motion sequencing (syncing transitions to nervous system cues).

This phase isn't about perfect execution. It's about trust—building a system that adapts without overthinking.

When It Lands

One client said it best: "For the first time, I didn't have to catch up to my own body. We were just... in sync." That's the goal. Not to perform calm. But to embody clarity. To stop buffering mid-movement or mid-thought. To stop adjusting every step. To let your system carry you—without hesitation.

Pause & Notice

- Do you feel like your brain and body are in the same rhythm?
- Or are you always one beat behind?
- Do simple tasks—reading, shifting, speaking—feel like more work than they should?

- What if that extra effort wasn't about willpower... but wiring?

When your system starts to sync, clarity doesn't have to be chased—it starts to arrive on its own.

Key Takeaways

You don't have to look clumsy to feel disconnected. When midline synchronization is off, even simple tasks like reading, reaching, or transitioning between thoughts can feel heavier than they should. It's not about effort—it's about wiring. Without clear communication between the left and right sides of the body and brain, coordination gets replaced by compensation. You move, think, and respond—but it takes more focus, more energy, more correction. That's not a lack of attention. It's a nervous system trying to function without a solid bridge.

The good news? That bridge can be rebuilt. Through cross-pattern movement, rhythm, and intentional sensory input, your system starts to sync. And when it does, clarity comes back. Focus takes less effort. Transitions feel smoother. Your body and brain stop negotiating every step—and start working as one. That's not just better coordination. That's integration.

CHAPTER 17

UNLOCKING FOCUS AND MEMORY

Miles was brilliant. A software engineer with a photographic memory and a dry wit that always landed with perfect timing —until recently. He still showed up early to sessions. Still tracked every habit. Still optimized his sleep, hydration, and caffeine intake with clinical precision. But something had shifted. "I feel like my brain's buffering all the time," he told me, eyes scanning the floor. "I'll be mid-sentence and forget where I'm going. I reread the same paragraph over and over—and none of it sticks."

He tapped his pen against his notebook—not fidgeting, just... trying to stay tethered. "It's not stress. I mean—it is—but not in the way it used to be. I'm not anxious. I'm not melting down. I'm just... off. Like my thoughts don't land where they're supposed to."

I nodded. I'd seen this before. His nervous system wasn't dysregulated in the way most people picture. He wasn't spiraling. He wasn't collapsing. He was simply living in a body that had lost the rhythm of connection. And the cost? Mental clarity. Focus. Memory. Not because he wasn't intelligent. But because his system couldn't hold onto what it already knew.

It Doesn't Always Look Like Chaos

When people think of dysregulation, they picture extremes—panic, rage, shutdown. But for many, it's subtler than that. It's forgetting why you walked into the room. It's losing your train of thought mid-sentence. It's rereading something important... and realizing you've absorbed none of it. It's buffering. Mentally. Emotionally. Systemically. And the frustrating part? You're aware of it the whole time. Your mind is sharp enough to know what's happening—but your body isn't anchoring the experience.

When the System Can't Hold What It Knows

I've worked with hundreds of people who live this way. They're driven. Organized. Thoughtful. The kind of people who highlight research studies, listen to podcasts at 1.5x speed, and optimize every part of their life. And still—their attention slips.

Their memory falters. Their execution lags behind their insight. They say: "I know exactly what I need to do. I just can't seem to stay with it." It's not a discipline issue. It's a dysregulation loop. And the body is always the missing variable.

Why Focus and Memory Aren't Just Mental

We're taught that attention is about effort. That recall is about intelligence. That if we just focus harder, plan better, or push through, we'll perform. But focus and memory aren't cognitive skills alone. They're physical. They're the result of well-regulated sensory systems, postural reflexes, and integrated movement patterns that keep the brain-body loop online.

When your nervous system is steady—focus flows. Memory holds. Tasks complete themselves. But when the nervous system is strained or disorganized—input floods in. Nothing sticks. And your brain burns through bandwidth just trying to keep up.

The Real Systems Behind Focus and Memory

Two brain systems sit at the center of this conversation:

1. The Reticular Activating System (RAS):

This brainstem-based filter decides what gets your attention and what doesn't. When it's regulated, it helps you tune out distractions, prioritize what matters, and stay present without effort. But when it's dysregulated, it's either hyperactive (everything feels loud, fast, overwhelming) or hypoactive (you feel foggy, flat, unreachable).

2. The Prefrontal Cortex (PFC):

The seat of executive function. This is where your working memory, task-switching, and follow-through live. But here's the kicker: the PFC can only operate when your lower brain systems aren't hijacking resources. You can't plan, recall, or reflect if your body is still in survival mode. And this is why so many people feel sharp—but scattered. Present—but not anchored.

When Focus Starts to Fray

Even if you consider yourself high-functioning, your system may be signaling strain through subtle patterns: you reread a paragraph three times and still can't remember it; you walk into a room, only to forget why you're there; you zone out mid-conversation and scramble to catch up; you lose track of your own thoughts while speaking. You use check-lists—not for planning—but because you know nothing will stay in your head otherwise.

You feel exhausted after trying to "focus" all day—without producing much. These aren't character flaws. They're symptoms of a system that's running too hot—or too fragmented—to hold attention efficiently.

When the Brain-Based Tools Don't Land

Meditation. Focus music. Nootropics. Breath work. These tools have their place. But they only work when the system is already regulated. When your body is overloaded, top-down tools fall flat. It's like trying to paint a house when the foundation is cracked. You don't need more mental hacks. You need a body that's capable of supporting the brain you already have.

How We Rewired Miles's System

Miles didn't need more motivation. He needed access. We started at the bottom—beneath thought, beneath planning, beneath performance.

Phase 1: Clear the Static

His sensory systems were firing on all cylinders. Too much visual tracking. Too little proprioceptive feedback. Too much scanning. We used: deep joint compression to quiet the body; vestibular resets like head turns and gentle rocking; tactile inputs that created body boundaries and restored a sense of "I'm here." His thoughts didn't immediately sharpen. But his breath dropped. His shoulders softened. And the background noise began to fade.

Phase 2: Anchor the Body

Miles didn't realize how unstable his system felt until we gave it something solid to land in. Breath-driven balance drills. Gaze anchoring while seated. Midline coordination exercises to restore symmetry and tracking. He started reporting fewer tangents. Less effort. More follow-through. "I don't lose the thread as often," he told me. "And when I do, I can find it again."

Phase 3: Build Communication Speed

With the interference gone and the foundation anchored, we rebuilt timing: cross-body crawling and marching, eye-hand tracking drills, call-and-response movement sequences tied to cognitive tasks. And then, something remarkable happened. He started remembering what he read —without rereading. He stopped avoiding creative tasks—because he wasn't afraid he'd blank. He had space in his mind again. Not because he forced it, because his body supported it.

From Overthinking to Integration

Miles wasn't chasing his thoughts anymore. They arrived. And they stayed. His productivity didn't just increase. His presence deepened. He stopped trying to remember what he was doing—and simply did it. This is what happens when focus becomes embodied.

What This Means for You

If you've ever felt like your brain can't hold onto a thought... If you rely on structure to survive your day... If you feel capable but not coherent... Please know: it's not a lack of intelligence. It's not laziness. It's not burnout from being "bad at focus." It's your body asking for regulation.

Pause & Notice

- Do you reread, rewind, or restart more than you want to admit?
- Do you try to think your way into focus—only to feel more scattered?
- Does your memory feel unreliable—even when things matter?
- Have you been chasing clarity... with a system that's never been shown how to anchor it?

Your clarity doesn't need to be earned. It needs to be supported. And the body already knows how to begin. Not through effort. Through rhythm. Through safety. Through connection.

Key Takeaways

Focus isn't something you force—it's something your system holds. When the body is overloaded or fragmented, even brilliant minds struggle to stay present. Rereading, zoning out, or losing your train of thought isn't a sign of weakness. It's a sign your nervous system is too taxed to support cognitive clarity.

Miles didn't need more mental tools. He needed less static in his system. Through rhythm, movement, and sensory feedback, we helped his body anchor what his brain already knew. And slowly, things shifted.

His thoughts stayed. His memory held. His mind stopped buffering—because his body finally felt safe enough to support it. That's the power of embodied focus: not more thinking, but deeper connection. Not mental hacks, but nervous system access. When regulation returns, clarity follows. Naturally.

CHAPTER 18

THE HIDDEN BARRIER TO MOTIVATION AND FOLLOW-THROUGH

M aya came in with fire in her eyes. She had vision. Ideas. Ambition. She could outline her five-year plan like a strategist. She had notebooks full of business ideas, color-coded habit trackers, and a whiteboard that looked like it belonged in a tech startup. "I'm not lacking clarity," she said, "I'm just... never getting traction." At first, I thought maybe it was burnout. But she wasn't exhausted. She was ready —or at least, she believed she should be. She cared deeply. She was articulate. Disciplined. Driven. But something wasn't landing.

Momentum slipped through her fingers. She'd get halfway through a project and lose steam. She'd sit down to write an email and stare at the screen until the words blurred. She'd light up in conversation... then go dark when it was time to follow through. "My drive shows up with a full tank—but my body's still stuck in park." And that's when I knew. This wasn't about procrastination. It wasn't a mindset issue. It was a nervous system that hadn't learned how to stay.

What Engagement Really Is

We're taught that if you want something badly enough, you'll make it happen. Push harder. Focus more. Hustle better. But that's not how engagement works. True engagement is not force. Its presence.

It's the nervous system saying, yes—and meaning it. It feels like: clarity without pressure, focus without strain, a body that stays rooted, even when the task gets hard, a mind that follows through, not because it has to—but because it can. When your system is regulated, engagement feels natural. When it's not, even simple tasks feel slippery. You start. But you can't stay.

When the System Pulls Away

Maya wasn't disinterested. She wasn't flaky. She wasn't lazy. She was dysregulated—in a way that didn't look dramatic, but felt paralyzing. And she's not alone. I've seen it in writers who open the document but never type. Coaches who map their programs but don't launch.

Parents who care deeply but feel numb at the dinner table. It's not lack of desire. It's lack of anchoring. Because when the nervous system feels unsafe, overwhelmed, or uncertain—it pulls back. Not to sabotage you. To protect you. It doesn't matter how exciting the task is. If the system doesn't feel stable enough to hold it, it will quietly drop it before you even know what happened.

What Engagement Looks Like in the Body

Engagement is more than attention. It's a full-body agreement to show up and stay. That agreement is built on three foundational systems:

1. Sensory Regulation – This is the system's ability to filter. When it's online, you can stay focused in noisy environments, handle distractions, and keep your mind clear. When it's offline? Every sound, sight, or shift becomes something your system has to survive. You can't focus on the task—because your brain is busy managing everything else.

2. Spatial Orientation – This is your body's map of itself. When the vestibular and proprioceptive systems are disorganized, your brain doesn't fully trust where you are in space. That low-level uncertainty reads as threat. And when something feels unsafe? The system won't invest. You'll check out—not because you're disinterested, but because you're trying to stabilize.

3. Motor Planning – This is the body's ability to organize itself for action. To sit down and begin. To stay through difficulty. To complete something complex without freezing or fleeing. When these systems aren't integrated, even small steps feel like heavy lifts.

This Isn't a Motivation Problem

You start projects but leave them open-ended. You feel scattered even when the plan is clear. You bounce between tabs, tasks, or ideas—without landing. You avoid the very thing you want, because you're afraid it'll feel too much. You feel ashamed for "checking out," but can't seem to stop it. You wake up with motivation—but it vanishes before noon. These aren't character flaws. They're nervous system patterns. And they can change.

What Maya Didn't Need

She didn't need a better planner. She didn't need morning affirmations or another cold plunge. She needed access. She needed her system to trust that staying wasn't going to cost her everything. And that's where the work began.

Rewiring Engagement from the Body Up

We didn't talk her into motivation. We trained her nervous system to stay anchored—so engagement could become a reflex, not a performance.

Phase 1: Reset the Signals

We started with stillness—but not silence. We gave her sensory systems something solid to lean on: ground-based proprioception—pressing her hands and feet into firm surfaces to reestablish body boundaries; vestibular resets—small, rhythmic head turns and rocking to signal "you're here, and it's okay to start"; patterned breath and movement—creating loops her system could trust. Her voice softened. Her gaze steadied. Tasks stopped feeling like cliffs.

Phase 2: Strengthen the Access Points

Next, we rebuilt the scaffolding for sustained attention: midline crossing drills to synchronize brain hemispheres, visual tracking to reduce jumpy, scattered perception, breath-body sequencing to match effort with regulation. She stopped checking out mid-task. She smiled. "I opened my laptop, and I didn't freeze."

Phase 3: Optimize Under Pressure

Once her system could stay present in the simple moments, we added light challenge: dual-task drills—balancing while solving puzzles; timed transitions—moving from one step to another with breath as the cue; progressive exposure—sitting with unfinished work, without shutting down. That's when the shift landed. She didn't just begin. She stayed.

The Real Win

It wasn't just that Maya finished the project. It was that she stopped fearing the process. She no longer interpreted difficulty as failure. She no longer mistook pauses for collapse. She didn't need to hustle to stay online. She said, "I finally feel like I can stay with myself." That's engagement. Not performance. Presence.

If You've Been Stuck in the Loop

If you've been blaming yourself for not following through... If your momentum feels more like luck than design... If you keep showing up, only to quietly check out...

Please hear this: you are not lazy. You are not scattered. You are not broken. Your nervous system just hasn't learned how to stay. And once it does? Motivation stops being a mystery. Execution stops being a fight. And showing up becomes something your whole system is built to hold.

Pause & Notice

- When does your energy drop?
- Do you freeze before starting—even when you care?

- Do you avoid finishing—not because it's hard, but because it feels too much?

Maybe the issue isn't your willpower, but your wiring—and maybe follow-through doesn't start in your mind at all, but in a body that finally feels safe enough to keep going.

Key Takeaways

Engagement isn't about pushing harder—it's about whether your system feels safe enough to stay. What looks like procrastination or flakiness is often a nervous system pattern rooted in disorientation, sensory overwhelm, or poor motor planning. When your brain doesn't trust your body to hold the task, it won't invest—no matter how motivated you feel.

This isn't a mindset problem. It's a regulation problem. And when you give your system the right input—rhythm, orientation, feedback—momentum stops being something you chase. It becomes something your body can finally sustain.

Because real follow-through doesn't start with a plan. It starts with presence.

CHAPTER 19

INTEGRATION, WHEN EVERYTHING STARTS TO WORK TOGETHER

There's a particular shift I've learned to spot. It's not loud. It doesn't announce itself. It arrives quietly, in the way someone exhales—like they didn't know they were holding their breath until it finally let go. It's not a breakthrough. Not a fix. Just the first moment when something inside them says: I'm okay right now. Not because everything's resolved. But because they're no longer bracing. That's what integration feels like. And more often than not, it doesn't show up the way people expect.

It shows up in the small ways: Someone walks across a room and doesn't scan the exits. They start a sentence—and finish it. They rest, and it feels like rest. They notice their breath dropped lower than usual and think: Wait... that was easy. They don't always have the language for it yet. But their system is already speaking it. Because integration isn't something you achieve. It's something your body remembers how to do.

The Real Goal Was Never Perfection

Let's be clear: this book has never asked you to be more disciplined. It hasn't told you to try harder, force calm, or perfect your routine. Because the point was never to master your nervous system. It was to meet it.

Integration isn't the reward for doing everything right. It's the result of finally giving your system the input it needed to work the way it was designed. Not optimized. Not upgraded. Just reconnected. When your reflexes support your posture... When your breath supports your attention... When your movement doesn't compete with your emotion... That's not a hack. That's a homecoming.

What Integration Actually Looks Like

Most people expect integration to feel like some kind of elevated state: more productivity, better focus, constant calm. But what it actually feels like... is less effort.

You walk into a room, and you're not tracking everyone's tone. You move from one task to another, and you don't feel like your thoughts fall out of your head. You experience stress—and your body doesn't tighten preemptively. You rest—and your system actually lets you. You don't need to micromanage your responses anymore. Your system starts to do it for you. That's what flow actually is.

Flow Isn't What You Think

In peak performance culture, we talk about flow like it's magic. That elusive zone of total clarity, speed, and creative momentum. Flow—at its core—isn't about magic. It's about capacity.

It's what happens when your internal resources match the demands of the moment. When your system says: "I know what to do." "I know where I am." "And I'm not afraid of what's next." You don't get there by pushing through. You get there by building the baseline. Because without regulation, flow doesn't land. It collapses. Or it burns you out.

When the System Can't Keep Up

I've worked with CEOs, teachers, parents, teens—people who could perform at an incredibly high level... for a time. But over and over again, I saw the same pattern: they couldn't sustain it. Because their nervous system was working harder than it should just to stay upright. When your system can't keep up with the input, everything feels harder.

You forget what you walked into the room for. You scroll endlessly, not because you're distracted—but because you're disconnected. You start avoiding even the things you care about, because your system flags everything as too much. And then come the stories: "I'm lazy." "I'm undisciplined." "I should be better than this." But the truth is: you were never designed to live in a constant mismatch between demand and capacity. And integration is what closes that gap.

You Can't Hack Your Way to Regulation

Most of the people I work with have already tried all the right things. They journal. They meditate. They biohack.

They optimize. But their body still holds tension. Still checks out at random moments. Still feels like it's missing something—like the pieces aren't syncing. Because no mindset, no affirmation, no morning routine can override a system that's still functioning in survival.

You can't affirm your way out of a vestibular gap. You can't gratitude-journal your way through a retained reflex. You can't schedule your way out of a sensory mismatch. You have to rebuild the circuit. And that's what this work does.

What Changes When Integration Lands

People often expect the shift to feel dramatic. But it usually feels like... relief. You don't dread transitions anymore. You don't rehearse every interaction in advance. You don't white-knuckle your way through the afternoon crash. And what comes instead is so simple it almost feels unbelievable:

You start things—and finish them. You feel your emotions—without spiraling. You sit still—not because you force it, but because your body allows it. You take a breath—and it reaches your belly. That's regulation. That's rhythm. That's the body returning to its baseline.

Integration Doesn't Mean Life Gets Easier

Let's not romanticize this. Life will still be life, and stress will still show up. You'll still have days where things fall apart. But you won't. Because integration isn't about avoiding difficulty. It's about your nervous system knowing how to recover.

You'll get dysregulated—and you'll find your way back. You'll lose focus —and know how to reset. You'll have a reaction—and know how to respond. That's the work. That's the win.

Where I've Seen It Land

I've seen a mother who couldn't tolerate noise from her kids... stand in the middle of a living room full of toys, music, chaos—and laugh. I've seen a college student who froze during every exam... take a test, finish early, and feel fine.

I've seen a therapist—who supported everyone but herself—finally say: "I don't feel like I'm faking calm anymore." Not one of them changed because they tried harder. They changed because their body finally learned how to hold what their mind already knew.

The Work Isn't Done. But It's Working.

Integration doesn't mean you're finished. It means your system is finally participating in the process. It means healing doesn't feel like a second job. It feels like a way of being.

You move through your day without constantly managing symptoms. You're not fighting your body anymore. You're moving with it. And slowly, you stop asking: "Am I doing this right?" Because the proof isn't in your performance. It's in your presence.

Pause & Notice

- What's different now? Not what you've mastered. Not what you've perfected. But what you've noticed.
- Do you feel your feet more on the floor?
- Do you remember to exhale before you react?
- Do you soften when you didn't mean to—and realize it felt good?

*These are the signs. Not of arrival. But of integration. And from here...
you don't perform your way forward. You follow the rhythm your body
now knows how to return to.*

Key Takeaways

Integration doesn't feel like a finish line. It feels like relief. It's not a
strategy or a routine—it's a nervous system that finally knows how to
recover without being told. You don't get there by perfecting your tools.
You get there by giving your body the input it was always missing:
rhythm, regulation, and safety in motion.

The real win isn't constant calm. It's the ability to return—without
spiraling. You don't force presence. You feel it. You don't chase flow.
You access it. That's what integration is: not something you achieve, but
something your system begins to remember. And from there... regulation stops being a project. It becomes the place you live.

PART IV

WHY LABELS ALONE DON'T LEAD TO LASTING CHANGE

By now, you've seen what happens when we stop chasing symptoms and start listening to the signals underneath them. You've learned that regulation isn't something you achieve with enough effort—it's something your body remembers when it's given the right inputs. You understand what it means to rewire, not with willpower, but with rhythm.

Now, we begin to look more closely at the patterns that often sit beneath those signals—the ones that shape how we move, feel, and cope in the world.

For some, these patterns showed up early. For others, they crept in slowly, hidden in the pace of survival. ADHD. Autism. Anxiety. Burnout. Sensory processing differences. Executive dysfunction. Emotional dysregulation. Traits that live under the umbrella of neurodivergence—a word that brings relief to some, stigma to others, and complexity to almost everyone who encounters it.

This part of the book isn't here to dismiss those labels. It's here to go underneath them—to explore what those labels are often trying to describe: a system that's been trying—brilliantly, creatively, and often invisibly—to survive without the regulation it was never taught to access.

Because the truth is, what we call a disorder is often a pattern. And that pattern didn't start in the mind. It started in the body.

You'll meet the children who couldn't sit still—not because they lacked self-control, but because their vestibular systems had never fully integrated. You'll meet the adults who struggled to follow through—not because they were unmotivated, but because their reflexes were still doing the heavy lifting their muscles weren't meant to carry.

You'll see what happens when sensory overload isn't seen as fragility, but as a sign of a system that never learned how to filter the world safely.

Neurodivergence is real. The challenges are real. But so is the possibility that we've been looking in the wrong place for solutions.

This part isn't about minimizing diagnosis—it's about expanding the conversation. Because insight doesn't equal access. And no amount of cognitive strategy will land if your body is still bracing underneath it.

Each chapter ahead will take one of these patterns—attention, sensory sensitivity, emotional volatility, low motivation—and reframe it through a body-first, brain-supported lens. Not to explain it away, but to offer a way through.

Because what looks like a deficit may be a defense. What looks like a lack of focus may be a lack of safety. And what we've been calling dysfunction may be adaptation—brilliant, resourceful, and ready to shift when given the right support.

It's where we stop asking "What's wrong with me?" and start asking "What does my system need to feel safe enough to change?" Because the brain might carry the label. But the body holds the solution.

Let's begin.

CHAPTER 20

ADHD, A BODY-FIRST
APPROACH

W e've been taught to see mental health through a diagnostic lens —ADHD, anxiety, autism, burnout. But what if these aren't personal failings? What if they're patterns of regulation—of energy, emotion, and engagement—that can be retrained? ADHD, for example, isn't just about attention. It's about regulation. That single shift changes everything. This section explores how a body-first approach reframes what we've been calling disorders—and offers a different path forward.

When Focus Isn't the Problem—Staying With It Is

Jillian was one of the most creative people I'd ever worked with. Ideas poured out of her like wildfire—bright, vivid, full of spark. But ask her to finish a single project, and the flame seemed to flicker. "I'll open my laptop to write," she told me, "and then suddenly I'm reorganizing the closet or looking up flights to places I'm not even going." She wasn't flaky. Or lazy. Or disinterested.

She was dysregulated. She'd been diagnosed with ADHD years earlier. Medication helped—sometimes. But the shame never left. The guilt of starting something and not finishing. The fear of being "too much" for the people around her. The exhaustion of masking her internal chaos behind polished presentations. She didn't need more effort. She needed more support. And not the kind that lived in apps, alarms, or rigid routines. She needed a nervous system that could help her hold the thread of her own focus.

The Misunderstood Nature of ADHD

ADHD isn't about not paying attention. It's about struggling to regulate attention—when to shift it, when to sustain it, when to let it go. While ADHD shows up differently for different people—some lean hyperactive, others inattentive, and many fluctuate between—the common thread is inconsistency. What's being regulated may vary, but what's struggling is the system itself.

For most of the people I work with, the issue isn't a lack of focus. It's a lack of access to the kind of focus they need, when they need it most.

One moment: hyper-fixation. The next: total blankness. It's not just distraction—it's time distortion. Task paralysis. Emotional impulsivity. Memory lapses. And more than anything, it's the unpredictability. That's what breaks people down. Not being "bad" at focus—but being brilliant one day and lost the next.

The Patterns Beneath the Diagnosis

Here's what ADHD often looks like from the inside: Inconsistent energy: One day, you're unstoppable. The next, you're watching the clock tick by, unable to begin. Overwhelm from minor tasks: An overflowing inbox can feel like a tsunami. Time dysregulation: Everything is either now or not now. Impulse without context: Decisions made in a flash, followed by waves of regret. Chronic underachievement: Despite intelligence. Despite effort. Despite care. Shame:

The kind that sinks in after every unfinished thing, every late form, every forgotten reply. This isn't about effort. It's about a nervous system that hasn't been wired for follow-through. And here's what no one tells you: The roots of ADHD live in the body, not just the brain.

Why Traditional Strategies Don't Stick

Jillian had tried it all. Calendar color codes. Task batching. Accountability coaches. Meditation. Medication. All of it helped. Until it didn't.

"I can focus on a system," she said once, "but I can't stay in one." And that's the rub. Systems are useful. But they're scaffolding. If the underlying structure isn't solid, they eventually collapse. Because you can't build cognitive control on top of a body that's still bracing.

A Body-First Look at ADHD

Before most people get diagnosed, their bodies are already trying to compensate. What looks like fidgeting, forgetfulness, or lack of discipline often starts much earlier—as sensory patterns, movement challenges, or missed developmental steps. Here's what shows up again and again in ADHD clients:

- **Poor Postural Control:** Constant shifting, leaning, needing to prop or brace.

- **Clumsiness:** Misjudging space. Knocking things over. Feeling off-center in motion.

- **Sensory Reactivity:** Overreacting to textures, lights, noise, or even too much quiet.

- **Motor Impulsivity:** Moving before processing. Talking before thinking.

- **Midline Integration:** Struggling with reading, tracking, crossing midline. Avoiding tasks that require spatial sequencing.

None of this is character driven. It's wiring.

ADHD as a Regulation Problem

ADHD isn't a motivation issue. It's a regulation issue—of energy, attention, timing, emotional tone, and spatial mapping. And regulation doesn't begin in the prefrontal cortex. It begins in the sensory systems. The proprioceptive system. The vestibular system. The reflex system. When those aren't integrated, focus becomes a fight. Stillness becomes a stressor. Memory feels like a sieve. And executive function lives on a delay.

The 3-Phase Framework

This is the approach we use with our clients—built on the same body-first foundation found in the book.

Phase 1: Reset – Anchor the Body That Can't Sit Still

We don't begin by forcing focus. We begin by helping the body feel safe enough to stop moving. For many ADHD clients, stillness doesn't feel restful—it feels unsafe. Their systems are constantly scanning, shifting, reacting.

So we start by anchoring the body through proprioceptive input: deep pressure, joint compression, and resistance-based movement that reinforces boundaries and restores a sense of "here I am." We add vestibular activation—rocking, spinning, and balance drills—to recalibrate spatial orientation, giving the brain a clearer map of where the body is in space. And we tie it together with core and breath sequencing, helping the system move from reactive motion to responsive regulation.

This isn't about stillness for stillness's sake. It's about showing the body that it can settle—and stay there—without losing itself.

Phase 2: Strengthen – Rewire Attention and Timing

Once the system feels safer, we begin strengthening the internal communication that supports sustained attention. Midline integration becomes a key focus—cross-body drills that build connectivity between the brain's hemispheres and reduce the mental lag that leads to zoning out.

When early movement patterns—like midline crossing, crawling, or coordinated bilateral tasks—are skipped or underdeveloped, the communication pathways that support executive function often remain incomplete. This shows up later as difficulty sequencing, following through, or shifting gears. Movement gaps in childhood become focus gaps in adulthood.

Visual-motor coordination trains the eyes to track, hold, and stabilize—supporting task initiation and reducing the jumpiness that often sabotages follow-through.

Finally, we layer in rhythmic sequencing: patterns of movement and timing that link the body's rhythm to cognitive pacing. These drills don't just build focus—they create fluency between intention and action. This is the phase where clients stop white-knuckling attention and start saying: "I'm actually finishing things. And it doesn't feel like a battle."

Phase 3: Integrate – Make Regulation Real-World Ready

In the final phase, we bring the work into the environments that matter most—classrooms, workspaces, homes. We introduce dual-task drills that combine movement with cognitive load, helping the system stay regulated even when life gets noisy. Executive sequencing takes the form of structured, layered tasks that require planning, shifting, and follow-through—mirroring the demands of daily life. And recovery circuits train the body to bounce back from activation quickly, without collapsing. This isn't just about staying calm. It's about staying capable.

We're not managing symptoms anymore. We're building a nervous system that sustains attention, adapts to change, and comes back online—on its own. Because regulation is about restoring the capacity to choose.

Two Stories That Still Stay with Me

Emma arrived with spreadsheets, alarms, and layers of internalized shame. "I feel like I'm smart on the inside," she told me, "but messy on the outside." When we started working together, she stopped trying to perform regulation and started practicing it—through crawling patterns, vestibular resets, and midline drills. She didn't force follow-through. She built it from the ground up. "I don't spiral when I get behind anymore," she said one day. "I just get back in."

Then there was Luca—a sophomore in college with a 135 IQ and a history of half finished assignments. He didn't lack insight. He lacked integration. So we stopped pushing his productivity—and started training his system. Two months in, he turned in his first paper early. "It's like my brain finally knows how to stay," he said. "I don't scatter the second something gets hard." That's not willpower. That's regulation.

Pause & Notice

- Do you forget things that matter—but remember things that don't?
- Do you toggle between hyper-focus and freeze?
- Do you find yourself working three times harder to do half as much—and blaming yourself for it?

These aren't flaws. They're signals from a system doing its best without a complete roadmap.

Key Takeaways

ADHD isn't a failure of focus. It's a nervous system that hasn't learned how to regulate the gears of attention—when to engage, when to pause, and when to return. What looks like distraction, inconsistency, or impulsivity often traces back to sensory disorganization, missed developmental sequences, or reflexes still stuck in survival. Your system adapted to survive—and it can adapt again, this time toward stability.

This chapter reframes ADHD not as a character flaw—but as a body-brain disconnect that can be rewired. When we stop managing symptoms from the top down and start restoring rhythm from the ground up, everything shifts. Focus flows. Tasks get finished. Regulation becomes reflex. Not because you tried harder—but because your system finally knows how to stay.

CHAPTER 21

AUTISM, A BODY-FIRST APPROACH

Noah didn't avoid people. He watched them. At three years old, he barely spoke. While other toddlers ran in chaotic loops, shouting over each other at the playground, Noah stayed still gripping a Matchbox car and spinning its wheels like the answer to something lived inside the rotation. He flinched at the sound of the vacuum, pulled at his socks with urgency. Refused new snacks, even ones his older sister loved.

When routines shifted, he cried—not out of defiance, but as if the world itself had gone off-axis. His parents were told he had autism. That he might never make eye contact. That connection would be something he'd always struggle with. That his nervous system needed to be "trained" to tolerate the world. But when he came into my office, I didn't see avoidance. I saw effort. The kind most people miss. I saw a body scanning, bracing, organizing the chaos of input with every ounce of energy it had. He wasn't afraid of people. He was trying to survive the volume of the moment.

When the Body Can't Track the World

Autism has long been described as a social and communication disorder. But those are surface-level symptoms. Underneath, what I see is a nervous system trying to interpret the world through a distorted map.

Sensory overload. Emotional shutdown. Movement rigidity. Delayed reactions.

These aren't behaviors to fix. They're adaptations. The body's best attempt at regulation in a world that doesn't line up with its internal signals. Before the first diagnosis, before the word "autistic" enters the conversation—the body has already been speaking.

What the Nervous System Was Saying All Along

In nearly every autistic individual I've worked with, there are early signs —not of pathology, but of patterns. Patterns that point not to broken- ness, but to disconnection between sensation, movement, and regula- tion. Motor milestones that arrive late—or never fully form. Crawling skipped. Toe-walking persisted. A wobble in balance that never quite resolves. Sensory extremes. Clothing tags feel like sandpaper. Back- ground sounds land like sirens.

Or the opposite—pain barely registers. Repetitive movement. Rocking, flapping, spinning—not for attention, but for self-organization. Emotional rigidity. A new cereal, a detour on the drive home, a substi- tute teacher—and the system crashes. These aren't quirks. They're signals. And they speak of a system doing its best to navigate the world with uncalibrated tools.

Why Top-Down Strategies Fall Short

Traditional approaches often start too far downstream—targeting the outward symptoms without addressing the internal systems that drive them. Teach eye contact. Coach conversational scripts. Reinforce behav- ioral "goals." But none of that lands if the body still feels unsafe.

You can't train connection into a system that's still stuck in survival. I've worked with autistic children who could memorize social phrases—but still collapsed after group time. I've worked with teens who could mask their discomfort—until they got home and went nonverbal from exhaustion. The performance was there. The connection was not.

What Happens When We Start at the Root

When we shift from behavior modification to body-based support, something changes. The goal stops being performance. It becomes safety. And from safety, something else emerges: availability. Because the real issue isn't a lack of interest in others. It's that their system can't process the interaction without bracing. Socialization isn't a skill to be forced. It's a state to be accessed—once the body can trust the experience.

A Body-First Framework for Autism Support

This approach isn't about changing autistic people. It's not about making anyone act neurotypical. It's about creating enough safety in the system for their true selves to come forward—fully, confidently, and sustainably. We don't aim for compliance. We aim for connection—through regulation. And we build that connection in three intentional phases.

The 3-Phase Framework

This is the approach we use with our clients—built on the same body-first foundation found in the book.

Phase 1: Reset – Ground the Senses

Before language, learning, or connection can happen, the nervous system needs to feel safe. For many autistic individuals, the world arrives in pieces—too much sound, too much light, too much motion, too many internal signals all at once. It's not about sensitivity. It's about overwhelm. The body isn't resisting connection—it's trying to survive sensation. So we start with input that calms the system from the bottom up. Vestibular tools like gentle rocking, linear movement, or slow spinning help the body trust space and motion. Proprioceptive input—joint compression, resistance bands, deep pressure—anchors the body to itself. Breath work and postural support reduce the noise inside the system, helping it come out of a constant defensive state.

The goal isn't focus or performance. It's a felt sense of safety. I am here. I am grounded. I don't have to brace. This is where regulation begins.

Phase 2: Strengthen – Build Predictability

Once the system feels more stable, we introduce pattern—not to promote rigidity, but to create safety through repetition. The autistic nervous system doesn't struggle with routine—it thrives on it. Because pattern reduces threat. Cross-body drills strengthen midline coordination and improve the brain's ability to communicate across hemispheres. Visual tracking and sequencing help organize input so the body can anticipate rather than react. Motor planning activities create confidence in movement and reduce the friction that comes from clumsiness or uncertainty.

This is where the system begins to feel organized from the inside. The world becomes more predictable—not because it changed, but because the body finally has a map. And when that predictability is in place, flexibility stops feeling threatening. The body no longer has to protect against the next unknown. It can move with it.

Phase 3: Integrate – Sustain Connection

With a grounded and patterned system, we can begin to build capacity —not through exposure therapy, but through gradual, body-led integration. We reintroduce sensory input—like light, noise, and social dynamics—in small, structured doses that the system can handle. Task transitions mimic real-life demands but are paced to prevent overwhelm. We layer in regulation drills that teach the body how to return to center after disruption—not by shutting down, but by recalibrating. The goal here isn't to push someone toward connection. It's to make connection sustainable. When the nervous system knows how to recover, it stops interpreting interaction as a threat. And that's when real engagement becomes possible—not because it's expected, but because it no longer feels like too much.

Carmen's Shift

Carmen was 18 and undiagnosed. She'd been called quiet. Shy. Awkward. She dreaded parties. Left messages unread. Needed hours to "reset" after a ten-minute phone call. Everyone thought she was introverted. She thought she was broken. Until we worked together. It wasn't about confidence. It was about capacity.

Her nervous system simply couldn't track conversation, body language, and social norms simultaneously. Her brain could—but her body burned out first. We didn't force eye contact. We didn't rehearse scripts. We rocked. Crawled. Rolled. We sequenced movements with breath. We anchored her gaze before we practiced transitions.

By month three, she joined a book club. By month four, she told me: "I didn't have to fake being okay. I actually enjoyed being there." She didn't just learn to participate. She learned to stay regulated inside participation.

The Goal Is Connection, Not Correction

This isn't about fixing autistic individuals. It's about giving them the internal stability to choose connection—on their terms. When you remove the sensory overwhelm... When you train the reflexes that support sequencing and safety... When you build a body that doesn't constantly feel like it's under siege... Connection doesn't feel like survival anymore—it becomes something sustainable. Even enjoyable. Not because the person has changed—but because the system finally supports who they've always been.

Pause & Notice

Maybe you're reading this as a parent. Maybe you're a provider. Or maybe you're someone who sees yourself in these words. If so, ask yourself:

- Do transitions drain you—even when the event seems small?
- Do you avoid interaction—not out of disinterest, but because your body can't keep up?
- Do sensory details—like lighting, volume, texture—impact your ability to stay engaged?
- Do you feel like you're always recovering from the world?

You don't need to force connection. You need a system that knows how to sustain it. The beautiful truth is, that system can be rebuilt.

Key Takeaways

Individuals aren't avoiding connection—they're often surviving input. What looks like withdrawal, rigidity, or disinterest is usually a system doing everything it can to stay regulated in a world that feels overwhelming. Traditional strategies often focus on behavior and performance, but the root issue is neurological—not motivational. When the body can't trust its sensory environment, connection feels like a threat—not a choice.

This is why top-down interventions often fall short. You can't coach social interaction into a body that's still bracing. But when we support the nervous system from the bottom up—through proprioception, vestibular input, patterning, and motor planning—something shifts. Regulation becomes possible. And from regulation, connection becomes sustainable.

Integration isn't about training someone to act neurotypical. It's about building enough internal safety for their true self to emerge. That's when connection becomes less about performance—and more about presence. Not because they were fixed. But because their system finally feels safe enough to stay.

CHAPTER 22

ANXIETY, A BODY-FIRST APPROACH

S ophia had lived with anxiety for as long as she could remember. Not the loud kind. Not the spiraling, gasping, dramatic panic she saw portrayed in movies. Her anxiety was quiet. Composed. Hidden. As a child, she was labeled "sensitive." Loud noises overwhelmed her. Sudden transitions turned her stomach. If a routine changed—if a substitute teacher walked in instead of her usual classroom guide—she would freeze. Her chest would tighten. Her jaw would lock. Everyone thought she was shy. But underneath the quiet was a system on high alert.

As an adult, not much changed. She could hold a job. Keep appointments. Navigate social settings. But her mornings began with a pounding heart and racing mind. Crowded rooms made her skin prickle. Small talk drained her—even when she wanted to connect. She tried all the right tools: mindfulness, journaling, reframing her thoughts. And yet, her body never stopped bracing. No matter how calm the moment, her system never fully believed it was safe.

What No One Told Her

Sophia had been taught that anxiety lived in her mind. That it was about overthinking. That if she just managed her thoughts better, the tension would go away.

But her experience said otherwise. Her worry wasn't rooted in logic—it was anchored in sensation. *What if?* didn't show up as a thought. It showed up as a buzz behind her eyes. A clench in her chest. A flutter beneath her ribcage.

And this is what I've heard from so many people like her—smart, thoughtful, high-functioning individuals who are exhausted from trying to "calm down" in a body that won't listen. They've done the work.

They've practiced the breathing. They've tried to reason their way out of their fear. But no matter how much their brain understands they're okay, their body refuses to believe it. Because anxiety doesn't begin in thought. It begins in regulation.

When the Nervous System Never Gets the Memo

We're in the middle of an anxiety epidemic. At the time of this writing, one in three adults in the U.S. reports experiencing anxiety. Children and teens are being diagnosed at twice the rate they were a decade ago. And despite all the new treatments, tools, and awareness, we're not seeing a shift.

Why? Because we've been trying to solve a body-based issue with brain-based tools. We've mistaken the signal for the source.

Anxiety isn't just excessive thinking. It's a nervous system stuck in high alert. It's like having a smoke alarm that won't stop blaring, despite there being no fire. The alarm isn't broken. It's just too sensitive. And no amount of reassurance will help until your body stops *hearing* danger.

That's why cognitive strategies often fall short. Until we teach the body how to come down, the mind can't truly let go of fear.

The First Signs Are Subtle

Before anxiety becomes a diagnosis, it whispers. Soft signs. The early cues that the system isn't settling. These are the clients who clench their jaw without realizing it, shift from foot to foot even when sitting still, hold their breath during conversations, startle easily, even at soft sounds, and feel overwhelmed in bright rooms or crowded stores. It doesn't look like panic. It looks like effort. Like their system is doing the job of bracing—all the time. And when I ask them if they feel safe in their own body, the answer is almost always: "I don't know how that's supposed to feel."

The Physiology of Fear

Anxiety is a full body experience. It lives in three primary systems—each playing a different role in how you sense safety, interpret danger, and stay present. One tracks input. One sets the rhythm. One builds the patterns. When they're aligned, the system adapts. When they're out of sync, anxiety becomes the default.

The Vestibular System – Balance, Orientation, and Internal Stability

Located deep within the inner ear, this system is often underestimated. But its influence reaches far beyond balance. The vestibular system tells your brain whether you're upright, moving, still, or falling. It's how your body knows where the ground is—and whether you're safe standing on it.

When this system is dysregulated, your body doesn't fully trust that it's steady. Even when you're standing still, you might feel off-balance. Foggy. Unsettled. Like gravity is unreliable. That low-level disorientation keeps your nervous system on edge, quietly scanning for threat—even if none is present. The result? A baseline of anxiety—not in your thoughts, but in your body's perception of space and safety.

The Proprioceptive System – Boundaries, Grounding, and Physical Presence

This system lives in your joints, muscles, and connective tissue—and it acts like an internal GPS. It tells your brain where your limbs are, how much pressure you're using, and how close you are to things around you. When it's underdeveloped or overwhelmed, your sense of body-in-space gets murky.

You may fidget constantly—not as a distraction, but as a way to feel anchored. You may press into objects, stretch, or shift often—not to move, but to confirm that you still exist inside your body. Without clear proprioceptive input, your nervous system can't settle. The edges of your experience feel blurry. Unclear. And that uncertainty feels like danger.

The Autonomic Nervous System – Regulation, Recovery, and Survival Readiness

This system governs how quickly you shift between states: calm, alert, activated, and shutdown. It determines whether your body responds to life as an experience—or as a threat. When stuck in a stress response—fight, flight, or freeze—your system stays braced. Muscles tighten. Breath shortens. Thought loops spin.

Even when the stress is over, the body doesn't always hear the 'all clear.' And when the other systems—vestibular and proprioceptive—aren't providing reliable input, the autonomic system remains on defense. Always scanning. Always preparing. Even in the absence of real danger.

This is why movement resets—like rocking, crawling, or deep pressure input—are so powerful. When used early, they can interrupt the spiral before it starts, sending safety signals through the body before the mind gets swept into fear.

What I Saw in Jordan

Jordan wasn't new to anxiety. He was 42. A software engineer. A dad. A husband. A reliable team member. But over time, his world had gotten smaller. He stopped flying. Stopped going to concerts. Avoided elevators and crowded spaces. He told me, "I used to be fine. Now I feel like my nervous system is allergic to life." He wasn't panicking. He was bracing. He showed up calm, composed, rational. But under the surface, his system was scanning. Preparing. Holding.

When we started body-based retraining, everything slowed down. Vestibular resets. Breath-led movement. Ground-based drills. And one day, it happened. He went to his daughter's recital. He sat through the whole performance. He didn't fidget. He didn't scan the exits. He didn't overheat or spiral or plan his escape. When I asked what felt different, he said: "I didn't have to survive the moment. I actually got to be in it." That's what regulation makes possible. Not just calm—but presence.

The 3-Phase Framework

This is the approach we use with our clients, built on the same body-first foundation found in the book.

Phase 1: Reset – Teach the System to Downshift

This isn't about forcing calm. It's about giving the system the sensory input it needs to stop bracing for danger. Before we can build resilience, we have to quiet the static. In anxious systems, the vestibular and proprioceptive circuits often misfire—leaving the brain without a reliable sense of where the body is in space. That's where we begin.

We use vestibular resets—gentle rocking, head turns, and orientation drills—to reestablish a baseline of safety in motion. Deep pressure inputs like joint compression and resistance exercises help the system feel its own edges again, reducing the floaty, ungrounded sensation many people live with. Finally, we restore internal control through breath and posture coordination—training the body to regulate from the inside out, rather than reacting from the outside in.

Phase 2: Strengthen – Build Reliable Body-Brain Communication

Once the system is less reactive, we begin improving how it processes and responds to input. Proprioceptive sequencing—intentional, resistive movements that train timing and spatial accuracy—helps the body feel more present and predictable.

We layer in rhythmic integration through cross-body patterns like tapping or crawling, which rewire pacing, anticipation, and internal rhythm. Visual-motor training rounds out this phase. By teaching the eyes to track, stabilize, and follow through, we quiet the static—so focus can return, especially under pressure. This is where the brain stops guessing what's safe—because the body is finally giving it a clear answer.

. . .

Phase 3: Integrate – Make Regulation Real

Now we apply regulation in motion—where life actually happens. We introduce light stress drills that challenge the system under manageable load: balancing while solving, switching between postures or directions with the breath as a guide. Transition practice helps the nervous system shift gears—moving from stillness to action and back—without triggering tension.

Finally, we train self-recovery with patterned sequences that help the body bounce back quickly after disruption. This isn't about staying calm all the time. It's about staying connected. Because anxiety isn't a failure of mindset—it's a signal that the system doesn't yet feel safe in movement, in change, or in stillness. And once it does? Regulation becomes something you don't have to chase. It becomes the place you return to.From

Bracing to Belonging

Sophia didn't stop worrying overnight. But she stopped bracing. Her shoulders came down. Her jaw softened. Her breath reached her belly. One morning, months into our work, she sat on her porch. No podcast. No task. No plan to escape the stillness. Just sunlight. Birds. Coffee. And calm. She said, "I felt like I was finally allowed to exist... without defending it." That's the kind of peace regulation brings. Not silence, but safety. Not escape, but return.

Pause & Notice

- Do you wake up already tense—before the day even begins?
- Do you feel overstimulated in ordinary environments?
- Do you overthink, not because you're anxious, but because your body won't settle?
- Do you want to rest—but never quite land?

This isn't about doing better. It's about understanding the signals beneath the surface. The patterns weren't the problem—they were the protection.

Key Takeaways

Anxiety isn't just a thought pattern—it's a full-body state. It doesn't always shout. Sometimes it whispers through jaw tension, breath-holding, restlessness, or the quiet urge to leave a moment—before it even begins. It's not weakness. It's your system doing its best with the signals it's been given. When the vestibular, proprioceptive, and autonomic systems are out of sync, your brain can't trust the environment—or your body's place within it. That's when anxiety becomes the baseline. Even in calm moments.

Sophia's story reminds us: insight isn't the missing piece—access is. You can know you're safe, and still not feel it. You can want stillness, and still brace against it. But with the right inputs—vestibular grounding, proprioceptive feedback, and breath-based regulation—the system begins to shift. Not because you forced it. Because it finally believes it's safe to let go.

Regulation doesn't erase fear. It anchors you through it. It gives your body a way back to presence. And that changes everything—not just how you move through the world, but how you experience yourself inside it.

CHAPTER 23

STRESS & BURNOUT, A BODY-FIRST APPROACH

Ava had always been the one people could count on—organized, composed, capable. She managed to build a successful career while raising three kids and running a household with machine-like precision. Late nights and early mornings were part of the deal, and pushing through was a skill she had long since mastered. She didn't complain—she coped. She got things done. Until, one day, she couldn't. It didn't start with a dramatic breakdown; it started with a dull, persistent fog. She began to lose her train of thought mid-sentence and would zone out during meetings she used to lead with ease. Minor irritations, like her partner loading the dishwasher "wrong," triggered outsized reactions. Everyday tasks felt monumental, and the big responsibilities felt completely out of reach.

Sleep became elusive. Caffeine became essential. Focus became a daily battle. The most terrifying part wasn't the exhaustion—it was the absence of bounce-back. Her usual tools—taking time off, going for walks, journaling, and resting—had no effect on the deep depletion she felt. Ava wasn't just tired. She was burned out. And nothing in her well-stocked toolkit was working. Because burnout isn't just about doing too much. It's about what happens when your system is bracing for too long—silently, repeatedly—without enough time to recover. It's not just overwork. It's depletion at the level of the nervous system.

The Burnout Epidemic We Can't Outperform

Burnout is no longer a rare affliction—it's the norm. According to Gallup (2023), 77% of employees report experiencing burnout at work. Over 75% of doctor visits are linked to chronic stress, as reported by the American Institute of Stress (2022). The World Health Organization now classifies burnout as a medical condition. Despite the proliferation of wellness programs, apps, and vacations, burnout continues to rise. Why? Because burnout is often misclassified as a time management issue when it's fundamentally a nervous system issue. Burnout doesn't begin in the mind—it begins in the body.

Before the Breakdown: The Body Whispers First

I've seen it in high-performing professionals who never miss a deadline—who lead teams, show up early, and seem composed on the outside. But under the surface, their systems are maxed out. They can deliver the presentation, but crash afterward. They smile in meetings but grind their teeth in sleep. They function through force—until they can't.

Long before burnout becomes a full-body shutdown, the nervous system sends quiet signals—whispers that something is off. Most people miss or dismiss them until it's too late. Common soft signs of systemic exhaustion include being wired at night but exhausted in the morning, and midday crashes that feel like shutdowns. You might notice forgetfulness or fog in conversation, snapping at minor irritations followed by guilt, frequent sighing or shallow breathing, a clenched jaw, or unexplained digestive discomfort.

These aren't signs of weakness—they're signs that your system is bracing constantly and has forgotten how to relax.

Why Traditional Strategies Don't Touch the Root

Conventional advice like "get more sleep," "take breaks," and "just say no" often fails in cases of burnout. These tips assume the body is still receptive to logical interventions. But in burnout, the logic center of the brain takes a back seat. The body isn't choosing to stay "on"—it has simply forgotten how to turn "off." Traditional stress relief tactics manage the calendar, not the nervous system. You can't schedule your way out of a body stuck in survival mode. You must retrain the signals.

Why Burnout Is a Nervous System Breakdown

Burnout is more than a lack of energy—it's a breakdown in regulation across three key systems.

The autonomic nervous system, which governs effort versus recovery, gets stuck in fight-or-flight even when no threat exists.

The proprioceptive system, responsible for internal body mapping, becomes weak, causing the body to overcompensate for posture and stability—resulting in more fatigue and less output.

The vestibular system, which handles balance and motion, when dysregulated, causes energy swings, mental fog, and overwhelm even in calm environments. When these systems lose harmony, the body becomes inefficient. Every action takes more energy, every recovery takes longer, and eventually, the tank runs dry.

Derek's Story: When the Drive Fades

Derek, a creative director who thrived under pressure, had always believed stress was his fuel. But over time, his go-to strategy stopped working. Missed emails, skipped meals, and forgetting names were the first signs.

Soon came panic attacks, memory lapses, and dizzy spells. "It's like someone unplugged me," he said. "And now I'm running on static." What Derek needed wasn't another motivational hack—he needed nervous system restoration.

His recovery began not with mindset, but with movement. His breakthrough was subtle: a single meeting attended fully, without zoning out or clenching his jaw. Presence, for the first time in months. That's the power of nervous system recalibration.

A Body-First Model for Burnout Recovery

This model isn't about quitting your job or disappearing into a retreat

—it's about restoring your body's ability to recover on a cellular, structural, and rhythmic level.

The 3-Phase Framework

This is the approach we use with our clients—built on the same body-first foundation found in the book.

Phase 1: Reset – Rebuild the Recovery Pathway

Burnout doesn't just deplete energy—it rewires the system to forget how to shut down. Many clients arrive in a state of chronic "on," where even rest feels like tension. The first step is rebuilding the body's access to "off." We begin with breath drills—specifically slow, diaphragmatic breathing paired with gentle resistance—to activate the parasympathetic system and create an internal cue of safety.

Ground-based movement provides structure for stillness: joint compression, and developmental patterns like crawling offer sensory feedback that helps the body feel contained, rather than scattered. We also introduce vestibular rebalancing—slow rocking, subtle balance shifts, and head-turn sequences—to reduce internal chaos and restore orientation. This phase isn't about relaxation. It's about giving the body permission to pause, without interpreting that pause as danger.

Phase 2: Strengthen – Build Capacity Without Collapse

Once the system can downshift, we begin rebuilding effort—without tipping into overdrive. Burned-out bodies often treat any demand as a threat, so we introduce input slowly, rhythmically, and predictably. Repetitive movement patterns—like rocking-to-standing drills or breath-to-step sequences—help the system anticipate effort without bracing.

Cross-body coordination rebuilds midline integration, reducing the brain's need to micromanage each motion and restoring fluidity between intention and action. Gait training, hand-eye drills, and motor sequencing reactivate communication between cognitive and physical systems—so that action feels aligned, not forced. This phase isn't about performance. It's about practicing effort in a way the nervous system can sustain.

Phase 3: Integrate – Make Recovery Automatic

In the final phase, we translate all that regulation and rhythm into real-world resilience. The goal isn't to remove stress—but to increase your system's ability to recover from it. We introduce dual-task drills that pair movement with mild cognitive load—like stepping while naming, balancing while recalling, or sequencing while shifting direction—to help the body stay regulated even under light challenge. Transitional circuits—such as moving from stillness to activity and back again—train the nervous system to shift gears without crashing.

And finally, we layer in self-regulation loops: micro-practices embedded into daily life that help the system return to baseline with minimal effort. Over time, recovery stops being a goal—and becomes a reflex. Not because stress disappears, but because the body no longer fears it.

Ava's Return to Herself

Several weeks into her body-first recovery, Ava sent a voice memo. She was folding laundry—once a task she rushed through in a fog. "I realized halfway through that I wasn't rushing," she said. "I wasn't fidgeting. I wasn't spiraling. I was just... present." There wasn't a dramatic break-through—just a quiet return. A return to a body that no longer felt hunted. A rhythm that could finally hold her. That's what recovery looks like. Not perfection, but presence.

Pause & Notice

- Do you feel wired and tired at the same time?
- Are simple tasks heavier than they should be?
- Have you rested without actually feeling restored?
- Are you still showing up—but feeling hollow inside?

These aren't motivational problems. They're nervous system signals. And the solution isn't more effort—it's new input. Input that tells your body: it's safe to stop bracing. You don't have to push through. You can come back.

Key Takeaways

Burnout isn't about weakness—it's about wiring. It happens when your system keeps accelerating without ever learning how to slow down. The first signs are subtle: effort that feels heavier than it should, rest that doesn't restore, and a growing sense that even the smallest tasks ask too much. This isn't a motivation problem—it's a regulation problem. And the solution isn't to push through or shut down. It's to retrain the system from the bottom up.

Through a body-first model, recovery becomes less about escape—and more about access. You stop chasing rest like a reward. You stop fearing demand like a threat. And you begin to build a system that can meet life without collapsing under it. This isn't about doing less. It's about doing what matters—without paying for it with your health.

Because real recovery isn't passive. It's practiced. And once your nervous system learns how to return, burnout stops being the end of the story. It becomes the turning point.

CHAPTER 24

NEURODIVERGENCE, THRIVING IN A DIFFERENTLY WIRED WORLD

Sam didn't struggle with intelligence. He was bright, wildly creative, and capable of diving deep into topics most people only skimmed. But traditional environments—classrooms, meetings, group conversations—felt too tight, too loud, or like being held underwater. From the outside, Sam looked restless, unfocused, disorganized. Inside, though, he was just trying to manage a system that wouldn't settle. His body was always in motion—tapping, shifting—not from distraction, but from necessity. He didn't lack motivation. He lacked a support system that actually matched how his body and brain worked.

By the time he turned fifteen, he'd been handed three different labels: ADHD, sensory processing disorder, and "mild" autism traits. None of them fully explained who he was. All of them framed what was "wrong," without asking what was missing. And what was missing... was regulation.

The Mismatch Between Wiring and Environment

Neurodivergence is too often defined by what's hard: attention challenges, sensory overload, disorganization, or social withdrawal. But these struggles often reflect a deeper mismatch—between how someone's system is wired and the world they're expected to navigate. Neurodivergence isn't a defect. It's a difference in how the nervous system processes input and organizes experience.

When that system is dysregulated, even the brightest minds can feel scattered, overstimulated, or shut down. Focus becomes a fight. Rest stays out of reach. Transitions feel like cliffs. And the support offered? Often too cognitive, too surface-level, too far downstream.

What I See Over and Over Again

By the time most neurodivergent clients reach my office, they're not just carrying diagnoses—they're carrying stories. Stories of trying to keep up while always feeling behind. Stories of being told to try harder, to focus more, to sit still, to be less. But underneath the coping strategies, I see the patterns that speak volumes. A body that can't stay seated without bracing. Shoulders that remain tight even during rest. Eyes that dart or glaze over when the pressure rises.

A nervous system stuck on high alert—even when nothing is wrong. These individuals aren't choosing to disengage. Their systems are doing the hard work of protection in environments that don't match their wiring. And the toll isn't just measured in productivity—it's measured in identity.

What Neurodivergence Looks Like in the Body

Forgetfulness, fidgeting, and frustration aren't personality flaws. They're signals of specific body-based breakdowns.

Sensory Integration Challenges: The world comes in too loud, too bright, or sometimes, too flat. Individuals crave deep pressure to feel grounded. They may flinch at certain sounds or lights and alternate between shutting down and overstimulating.

Vestibular and Proprioceptive Instability: The brain struggles to locate the body in space. This can show up as feeling floaty, unsteady, or having poor posture and chronic restlessness. Still environments, oddly enough, can be the hardest places to focus.

Midline Disconnection: When the brain's left and right hemispheres aren't syncing, people may struggle with sequencing, task tracking, and fluid transitions. They might switch hands mid-sentence or lose rhythm mid-task.

A Story That Stayed With Me

Isabel was 32, a brilliant artist and thinker, always alive with insight, but always drained. Every interaction seemed to cost her something. Every group effort felt like survival. She could hold it together, but it took everything she had. "I feel like I'm acting in a play I didn't audition for," she told me. "I'm always playing myself—but it's never actually me." We didn't coach her to mask better. We didn't hand her more scripts or planners.

We gave her nervous system new patterns—vestibular drills, breath-led movement, cross-body coordination, and rhythmic pacing. Slowly, her system stopped bracing. Her energy came back. Her voice, once filtered through the lens of survival, began to emerge naturally. Not because she was trying harder—but because she didn't have to anymore.

Why Traditional Supports Fall Short

Most neurodivergent supports are cognitive. Tools like color-coded planners, timers, prompts, visual schedules, and social stories are helpful scaffolds—but they don't rebuild the body's foundation. Because the issue isn't always rooted in executive function—it's often rooted in body function.

If the nervous system is dysregulated, no amount of organization will stick. The moment pressure hits, the body defaults to survival mode. That's why we need more than mental tools—we need somatic safety.

A Body-First Framework for Neurodivergent Regulation

This work doesn't aim to "fix" neurodivergence. It exists to help the body carry difference—without collapsing under its weight.

The 3-Phase Framework

This is the approach we use with our clients—built on the same body-first foundation found in the book.

· · ·

Phase 1: Reset – Return to Baseline

Before we can expect focus, presence, or flexibility, we need a nervous system that feels steady in its own body. That's where we start. In dysregulated systems—especially those shaped by sensory sensitivity, anxiety, or neurodivergence—the first priority is downshifting from chronic alertness.

We use vestibular inputs like gentle rocking, rolling, and spinning to restore a sense of spatial stability. Deep pressure through joint compression or weighted input calms the sensory field and helps the body re-establish its own boundaries. Breath and postural drills reconnect internal rhythm with external presence, teaching the system not just how to calm down—but how to come home.

Phase 2: Strengthen – Build Body-Brain Communication

With the system calmer and more grounded, we turn toward clarity. This phase strengthens the internal coordination that helps the brain and body move as a team. Cross-body movement patterns create left-right integration: they make it easier to focus, shift, and respond. Rhythmic drills reintroduce timing and sequencing, helping the system predict what's coming next without freezing or flinching. Eye-tracking exercises refine spatial orientation and reduce cognitive overload, so transitions stop feeling jarring.

This is where presence gets easier—not because the world quiets down, but because the system can now filter what matters.

Phase 3: Integrate – Apply in Real Life

This is where we bring the work into motion. Because calm doesn't matter if it can't hold in the middle of life. In this final phase, we layer dual-task drills: gentle cognitive challenges paired with movement—designed to help the system practice regulation under mild stress.

We explore emotional pacing through breath-synced movement, helping the body stay present through intensity without tipping into shutdown. And we build in real-time recovery sequences, so the system doesn't just avoid spirals—but knows how to return from them. This is where regulation becomes reflex. Not something you perform—but something your body remembers how to do.

From Surviving to Belonging

Sam didn't need to be more focused, less sensitive, or better at conforming. He needed a system that could hold space for how he already was. Once he stopped fighting his wiring and started supporting it, everything changed.

Fidgeting remained. So did his need for rest after intense interactions.

But he wasn't drowning anymore. He could stay present with himself—through transitions, conversations, and challenges. Not because he learned to hide better. But because his system finally knew how to stay.

Pause & Notice

- Do you find yourself burning out faster than others?
- Do you need more rest, space, or silence—but feel guilty asking for it?
- Does your mind race ahead while your body lags behind?

What you're noticing isn't weakness—it's information. The body isn't malfunctioning; it's messaging. And when you begin to support your nervous system instead of overriding it, something shifts. You stop chasing capacity and start creating it—through calm, through clarity, and through a system that finally feels safe enough to hold you.

Key Takeaways

The challenge isn't how someone thinks—it's what their system is being asked to carry.

When the nervous system lacks regulation, even the most capable individuals can feel scattered, overstimulated, or on edge. It's not a mindset issue—it's a mismatch between internal wiring and external demands.

What looks like distraction, disorganization, or delay is often the body's response to unfiltered input, unstable grounding, and sensory overload. These patterns aren't flaws. They're feedback.

You don't create regulation by forcing focus. You create it by rebuilding the systems that support it—from the body up.

And when those systems are restored, something shifts: the pressure eases, clarity returns, and the nervous system stops surviving the moment—and starts participating in it.

CONCLUSION

When the Body Leads, the Brain Follows

This isn't the end. It's the beginning. By now, you've seen what happens when we stop treating mental health as a mindset problem—and start honoring it as a conversation between body and brain. You've walked alongside the stories. You've listened to the signals. You've witnessed what becomes possible when regulation becomes the goal—not perfection.

This work doesn't ask you to push harder. It invites you to feel safer. Where effort once felt like survival, you now know it can become rhythm. Where symptoms once felt random, you now recognize them as signals. Where self-blame once lived, you've planted something new: a nervous system learning to trust again. And trust always begins in the body.

You remember Adam—the boy who couldn't sit still. He didn't heal by suppressing his movement. He healed by trusting it. Through rhythm, weight, and breath, his body found its anchor. And when the motion settled, the mind followed. You remember Diana—who once called stillness a form of exile. Now, she calls it home. Neither of them changed because someone told them to "calm down." They changed because their systems were shown how. Not through performance, but through presence. Through movement. Through rhythm. Through breath.

This is your work now. Start with the ground beneath your feet. With the breath rising in your belly. With the one small movement that says, *I'm here. I'm listening.* You don't have to chase calm. You don't have to earn your rest. You don't have to fix what was never broken. You only have to remember what safety feels like—and let your body lead the way back. Because when the body leads, the brain follows. And when your nervous system feels safe, everything else becomes possible again.

Where Insight Becomes Integration

If you're ready to keep moving forward, the LifeBoat App is here to meet you. More than a checklist, LifeBoat is your guided companion and digital on-demand workbook—offering simple movements, daily resets, and real-time reminders that your body already knows the way home. You don't have to journey alone. Healing is not just an idea. It's a rhythm. It's a practice. It's life.

Scan the QR code to step into LifeBoat, a space where insight becomes rhythm—and rhythm becomes resilience.

•••

MY REASON WHY

This work began long before I had words for it. It started in dusty barns, with horses who couldn't lie. It grew in quiet rooms with children whose bodies spoke louder than their voices. It deepened every time I sat across from someone trying to think their way out of pain—and saw, instead, a body asking for help.

I didn't write this book because I had all the answers. I wrote it because I saw too many people blaming themselves for systems that had never been shown another way. I wrote it for the ones who know all the right steps but still wake up braced for battle. For those who learned to survive before they ever learned to trust. For the ones whose resilience was never the problem—only the wiring underneath it. If that's you, know this: you are not broken. You are not failing. You are not alone.

Your body has been trying to tell the truth all along. And now, you have a map to listen to it—and lead with it—differently. he future of mental health won't be built by harder thinking. It will be shaped by those willing to honor the body's wisdom first: to move, to breathe, and to trust their way back to regulation.

It will be built by those brave enough to believe that healing isn't a battle to win. It's a rhythm to return to.

If this book has given you even one moment of recognition—one breath, one shift, one glimpse of what's possible—then it has done its work. I'm deeply grateful you chose to share this part of your journey here. More than anything, I hope you carry this truth with you:

You were never as far from healing as you feared. And when the body leads, the brain follows.

Thank you for listening to your body—and choosing to follow.

— Dr. Jim Costello

GLOSSARY

Body-First Regulation™

The foundational approach.

A bottom-up model for nervous system regulation that begins in the body—not the brain. It uses movement, breath, posture, and rhythm to restore safety before cognitive tools can take hold.

Bracing

A subtle, ongoing tension in the body—like holding your breath or clenching muscles—often triggered by stress or uncertainty. It's your body's way of staying ready, even when your brain says everything's fine.

Cerebellum

The part of the brain that helps control balance, coordination, and fine motor movement. It plays a key role in how the body learns rhythm and maintains postural control—critical for regulation.

Co-Regulation

When your nervous system settles in response to someone else's calm, steady presence. Often the first step before learning to self-regulate.

Corpus Callosum

The bundle of nerve fibers that connects the left and right sides of the brain. It allows both hemispheres to communicate and coordinate. Activities that cross the midline—like crawling or cross-body movements—help strengthen this connection, supporting learning, attention, and regulation.

Costello Framework

The clinical structure.

A 9-step framework that guides the practical application of the Costello Method™. It sequences movement-based inputs like rhythm, reflex integration, breath, and posture to systematically rebuild regulation from the ground up.

Costello Method™

The whole system.

A comprehensive, body-first approach to nervous system regulation rooted in movement science, developmental neurology, and subcortical repair. It includes the philosophy, tools, clinical applications, and delivery models (e.g., LifeBoat, coaching, programs).

Cortex

The "thinking brain"—responsible for language, logic, planning, and self-reflection. It often gets overridden when the body is dysregulated.

Dysregulation

A state where your nervous system is stuck in fight, flight, freeze, or shutdown. It becomes hard to think clearly, stay calm, or connect with others.

Fight / Flight / Freeze

Survival responses wired into your nervous system. Fight means gearing up for conflict, flight means escaping, and freeze means shutting down or going numb when overwhelmed.

HRV (Heart Rate Variability)

A measure of how much time varies between heartbeats. Higher HRV usually means your nervous system is more flexible and resilient—able to shift between stress and recovery. It's one of the most reliable indicators of nervous system health.

Hypervigilance

A state of constant alertness where your nervous system is always scanning for threat—even when no real danger is present. Often shows up as tension, jumpiness, overreaction, or difficulty relaxing. It's not paranoia —it's protection.

Integration

The process of connecting and coordinating parts of the nervous system, brain, or body that may have been working in isolation. In this book, it often refers to integrating primitive reflexes or sensory input so the system can move more fluidly and flexibly between states.

Interoception

Your ability to sense internal body signals—like hunger, heartbeat, or the need to breathe. It's how your body tracks what's happening inside, and it plays a key role in emotional regulation.

Limbic System

The emotional and memory center of the brain. It interprets danger, stores emotional experiences, and influences how you react to stress.

Maladaptive Plasticity

When the brain adapts to stress or trauma in ways that help you survive short-term, but limit long-term regulation, flexibility, or calm.

Midline

The invisible line that runs down the center of your body—from head to pelvis. Developing awareness and control across the midline is essential for balance, coordination, and integration between the left and right sides of the brain and body. Many reflex patterns depend on strong midline activation to support regulation.

Nervous System Regulation

The ability to shift between alertness, calm, rest, or action—and return to balance after stress. True regulation is flexible, not forced.

Neuro-Balance Quiz™

The entry point.

A personalized assessment that identifies a person's dominant Regulation Style™—a pattern of nervous system function that influences behavior, emotion, and resilience. It helps individuals find their starting point within the Costello Method.

Neurodivergence

A term that describes natural variations in how people think, feel, move, and process the world. Includes ADHD, autism, sensory sensitivity, and other brain-based differences. Neurodivergence is not a defect—it's a difference in wiring.

Neuroplasticity

The brain's ability to change and rewire based on experience. It's what makes healing possible—especially through movement, rhythm, and input.

Neuroreformation™

The paradigm shift.

A broader reimagining of mental health that moves away from top-down, insight-driven models and centers the nervous system as the starting point for lasting change. It's the philosophical and clinical backbone of The Costello Method.

Parasympathetic Nervous System

The part of your nervous system responsible for rest, digestion, and recovery. It helps your body downshift after stress and return to a state of calm, connection, and restoration.

Pattern

A body-based survival response shaped by experience, often expressed through behavior, movement, or emotional reactivity. In this book, patterns are not seen as flaws—but as adaptations the nervous system developed in response to dysregulation or threat. What looks like distraction, shutdown, or volatility may actually be a system doing its best to stay safe.

Postural Reflexes

Automatic, body-based responses that help you stay upright and balanced. If they're unintegrated, they can impact coordination, focus, and emotional steadiness.

Prefrontal Cortex

The part of the brain involved in decision-making, attention, emotional regulation, and social behavior. It functions best when your nervous system feels safe. Under stress, it tends to go "offline," making it harder to think, speak, or connect.

Primitive Reflexes

Involuntary movement patterns present at birth—like the startle or grasp reflex. These are meant to fade as the brain develops, but if they stay active, they can interfere with behavior and regulation.

Proprioception

Your internal body awareness—how you know where your limbs are, how much pressure you're using, and whether you're balanced. It's essential for movement and feeling grounded.

Reflex Resets

Specific movements that help complete and calm primitive reflexes still active in the body. They're a way to bring your system out of protection and back into balance.

Regulation

The body's ability to respond to stress and return to calm without getting stuck in survival mode. It's not about being calm all the time—it's about recovering quickly and safely.

Regulation Engine

A term used to describe the integrated system of reflexes, postural responses, and sensory pathways that supports self-regulation. When this engine is out of sync, the system stays stuck in survival. When it's online, the body can access calm, focus, and resilience.

Regulation Style™

The personalization lens.

A body-based pattern that describes how a person experiences and recovers from dysregulation (e.g., Overactive, Underconnected, Mixed). Used to tailor movement protocols and track regulation over time.

Reticular Activating System (RAS)

A part of the brainstem that controls alertness and filters what sensory input gets your attention. When overactive, it can keep you overstimulated or scattered.

Rhythm

The natural timing, pacing, and sequencing the nervous system uses to organize itself. In this book, rhythm is the foundation of regulation—it's how the body returns to balance. Where force fails, rhythm restores. It shows up in movement, breath, and sensory input—and becomes the language of safety when words fall short.

Sensory Input

Information your body receives through touch, sound, sight, pressure, movement, and space. It shapes how your nervous system feels—safe or on edge.

Sensory Integration

The brain's ability to organize and respond to input from the senses. When this process is disrupted, it can cause overreaction, underreaction, or confusion in everyday situations.

Sensory Mismatch

A disconnect between what the body expects and what it actually experiences—often triggering dysregulation. Common in sensory processing differences.

Subcortex

The fast, instinctive part of the brain that manages survival responses, movement, and reflexes. It reacts before conscious thought—and is often running the show under stress.

Sympathetic Nervous System

The part of your nervous system that activates during stress. It powers your fight-or-flight response—increasing heart rate, sharpening focus, and preparing your body for action. Useful short-term, but exhausting if always on.

System Override Sequence

A quick sequence of body-based movements designed to shift the nervous system out of a dysregulated state. It gives the body an "off-ramp" from stress by using movement and rhythm to reset the system from the bottom up.

Top-Down vs. Bottom-Up

Top-down means trying to change how you feel through thought (like reframing or mindset). Bottom-up means starting with the body—using movement, breath, or sensation to shift the nervous system. This book focuses on the latter.

Vagus Nerve / Vagal Activation

A nerve that runs from the brainstem to the gut, heart, and lungs. Stimulating it (via breath, movement, or pressure) helps shift the body out of stress and into a calm, connected state.

Vestibular System

The inner ear system that helps your body sense motion, balance, and spatial orientation. When regulated, it supports calm and coordination. When off, it can make the body feel unsteady—triggering fidgeting, anxiety, or sensory overload.

REGULATION REWIRED: BODY-FIRST VS. BRAIN-FIRST

Most people are taught to start with their thoughts—reframing beliefs, practicing mindfulness, analyzing behavior. These brain-first tools can offer moments of clarity, especially when the nervous system is already regulated. But when your system is stuck in survival—bracing, overwhelmed, or shut down—insight alone isn't enough to create change.

That's because regulation doesn't start in the mind. It starts with input —movement, rhythm, breath, and sensory signal. These are the body's first language, the signals that shape what the brain perceives as safe or dangerous.

This is the foundation of The Costello Method™, a 3-phase system built on developmental movement and rhythm. It's also part of a broader model we call Bottom-Up Neuroreformation™—a reimagining of mental health that doesn't begin with mindset, but with access.

The chart below compares these two approaches—Body-First Regulation and Brain-First Strategy—so you can understand what your system might actually need. If insight hasn't been enough, you're not doing it wrong. You may just need a different starting point.

Core Belief

Body-First: *"The body leads. The brain follows."*

Brain-First: *"If I think better, I'll feel better."*

Where Regulation Starts

Body-First: In the subcortex—through movement, rhythm, and sensory input.

Brain-First: In the cortex—through insight, analysis, and conscious control.

Main Focus

Body-First: Your regulation style—how your body reacts to stress, noise, or touch.

Brain-First: Thoughts, beliefs, and cognitive distortions.

How it Begins

Body-First: Meets you through rhythm, movement, and sensory experience—especially when words fall short.

Brain-First: Meets you through language, insight, and cognitive reflection—when the mind is calm enough to engage.

First Step

Body-First: Breath, posture, balance, rhythm.

Brain-First: Reflection, logic, and planning.

Where it Breaks Down

Body-First: Overwhelm, shutdown, or hidden nervous system stress.

Brain-First: When "knowing better" doesn't create change.

What Others May Assume

Body-First: Lazy, avoidant, or not trying hard enough.

Brain-First: Overthinking, or stuck "in their head."

Best For

Body-First: People who feel stuck even with insight or therapy.

Brain-First: People who can regulate once they reframe.

End Result

Body-First: Sustainable regulation—even under stress.

Brain-First: Mental clarity that may not translate into action.

Closing Note

Understanding these two models can help you choose the right tools at the right time. If insight alone hasn't been enough, you're not broken—you may just need to start from the bottom up.

The Costello Method™, grounded in Body-First Regulation™, reflects a deeper truth: lasting regulation starts in the body. Only then can the brain follow.

FAQ'S

Frequently Asked Questions about The Costello Method

Whether you're just discovering body-first regulation or you've tried every mindset tool without lasting change, these questions help clarify how The Costello Method works—and why it may be the missing piece you've been looking for.

What makes The Costello Method different from other nervous system tools?

Most methods start with the mind—reframing thoughts, managing behavior, or calming down through willpower. The Costello Method starts with the body. By engaging movement, breath, and rhythm, it works directly with the subcortical systems that shape regulation. It helps the body feel safe, so the brain can finally catch up.

Is this the same as somatic therapy or body-based mindfulness?

Not exactly. While both approaches acknowledge the body, The Costello Method is built on structured developmental movement that activates the brain-body connection through neuroplasticity. It's not just about sensing the body—it's about restoring the foundational reflex and rhythm patterns that support lasting regulation.

Do I need to be fit, flexible, or athletic to do this work?

Not at all. These movements are gentle, accessible, and designed to meet your nervous system—not your fitness level. Whether you're lying on the floor, seated in a chair, or adapting movements for your body's capacity, the input is what matters—not the form.

How quickly can I expect to feel a difference?

Some people feel subtle shifts—like better sleep, less tension, or emotional steadiness—within the first few sessions. For others, it takes a few weeks of consistent practice. Like anything rooted in biology, the results are cumulative. Slow and steady rewires the system.

Can I use this alongside therapy or medication?

Absolutely. The Costello Method is a complementary tool—it helps therapy land more deeply and can reduce the baseline stress that medications often target. It's not a replacement for clinical care, but it helps the nervous system become more responsive to it.

Is this safe for children or neurodivergent individuals?

Yes. In fact, it's particularly effective for children, teens, and individuals with ADHD, autism, or sensory challenges—because it bypasses verbal processing and works directly with the systems that support regulation. It's a non-invasive, movement-based approach that meets them where they are.

What if I feel worse before I feel better?

That can happen. When your system starts to shift, it may temporarily unearth stored tension or emotion. This doesn't mean something is wrong—it means something is moving. Go slow. Use grounding tools like wall presses or foot pressure. Your job isn't to push—it's to listen.

Is this a replacement for therapy or diagnosis?

No. The Costello Method is a powerful support tool, but it's not a substitute for mental health treatment, trauma-informed care, or medical guidance. It's a framework that helps your body feel safe—so that other supports can work better, too.

REFERENCES & FURTHER READING

This section offers a curated collection of scientific studies, clinical resources, and leading books that support the nervous system–based approach explored throughout this book. If you're curious to dig deeper into neuroplasticity, sensory processing, movement-based therapy, or body-brain integration, these resources provide a strong foundation for continued learning.

Neuroscience & the Body-Brain Connection

Doidge, N. (2015). The Brain's Way of Healing. Viking.

Explores how the brain rewires through movement, rhythm, and sensory input.

Siegel, D. J. (2012). The Developing Mind. The Guilford Press.

Demonstrates how body-brain integration shapes emotional and cognitive development.

Porges, S. W. (2011). The Polyvagal Theory. W.W. Norton.

Reframes how vagal tone influences stress responses, regulation, and connection.

Ratey, J. J. (2008). Spark. Little, Brown.

Outlines the science behind movement and cognitive performance.

Nervous System Regulation & Emotional Resilience

Levine, P. A. (1997). Waking the Tiger. North Atlantic Books.

Introduces somatic approaches to trauma and nervous system recovery.

Van der Kolk, B. (2014). The Body Keeps the Score. Viking.

A foundational text on how trauma lives in the body and what heals it.

Hanson, R. (2013). Hardwiring Happiness. Harmony.

A practical guide to neuroplasticity and emotional retraining.

Sensory Processing & Movement-Based Therapy

Ayres, A. J. (2005). Sensory Integration and the Child. Western Psychological Services.

Foundational work on sensory integration theory.

Blomberg, H. (2015). Movements That Heal. BookLocker.

Details how early motor patterns influence brain development and self-regulation.

Berlucchi, G., & Aglioti, S. M. (2010). The Body in the Brain. Oxford University Press.

Explores how the brain processes movement, sensation, and spatial perception.

Cognitive Performance & Focus Training

Medina, J. (2014). Brain Rules. Pear Press.

A user-friendly overview of how the brain thrives through sleep, movement, and focused work.

Gazzaley, A., & Rosen, L. D. (2016). The Distracted Mind. MIT Press.

Details how modern life interferes with attention—and what supports it.

Diamond, A. (2013). Executive Functions. Annual Review of Psychology, 64, 135–168.

An academic but accessible look at focus, memory, and executive control.

Balance, Coordination & Brain Synchronization

Shumway-Cook, A., & Woollacott, M. H. (2017). Motor Control. Lippincott.

Translates movement science into clinical practice for neuro-motor development.

Clark, J. E., & Metcalfe, J. S. (2002). The Mountain of Motor Development. Research Quarterly, 73(1), 20–25.

A metaphor for how movement builds developmental foundations.

Kleim, J. A., & Jones, T. A. (2008). Principles of Experience-Dependent Plasticity. Journal of Speech, Language, and Hearing Research, 51(1), S225–S239.

A key piece on how repetition and experience reshape the nervous system.

Vagus Nerve Stimulation & Stress Recovery

D'Andrea, W., et al. (2013). Physiological Response to Trauma Reminders. Journal of Traumatic Stress, 26(2), 192–200.

Explores vagus nerve function in trauma response.

Craig, A. D. (2002). Interoception: The Sense of the Body. Nature Reviews Neuroscience, 3(8), 655–666.

Explains the role of internal body awareness in emotion regulation.

Burgess, J. W., & Benedek, D. M. (2020). Vagus Nerve Stimulation in PTSD. Current Psychiatry Reports, 22(8), 45.

Reviews clinical uses of vagus nerve stimulation for emotional regulation.

Community, Mindset & Lifelong Integration

McGonigal, K. (2015). The Upside of Stress. Avery.

Redefines stress as a growth tool when approached with support and strategy.

Lieberman, M. D. (2013). Social. Crown.

Outlines how the brain is wired for connection—and how community accelerates change.

Dweck, C. S. (2006). Mindset. Random House.

The cornerstone of growth mindset thinking—especially relevant to neuroplastic change.

Final Thoughts: Nervous System Rewiring

These studies and resources form the foundation of the Costello Method—a science-based, movement-driven approach to mental wellness.

As you've read, this process isn't about pushing through symptoms or managing dysfunction. It's about restoring the signals that allow your system to adapt, focus, and recover—naturally.

This work isn't about fixing what's wrong. It's about remembering what your body already knows—and giving it the tools to return to flow.

ABOUT THE AUTHOR

Dr. Jim Costello is a clinician, educator, and founder of Neuro-Fit Systems. He developed The Costello Method™—a body-first system for rewiring the stress response through movement, rhythm, and nervous system repair. His work challenges the idea that mental health is a mindset problem. Instead, it reframes it as a physiological pattern—something we can access, shift, and rebuild.

As the originator of Body-First Regulation™ and Neuroreformation™, Dr. Costello starts where most mental health models end: with the body. His 9-step method helps people rewire regulation at the root —through breath, posture, reflexes, and rhythm—not through willpower, but through access.

Used by neurodivergent kids, elite performers, and overwhelmed professionals alike, his approach reaches the people traditional models often leave behind. Through the LifeBoat app and live programs, he offers more than tools—he offers a new map. Because when the body is safe, the brain doesn't have to fight. It follows.

For more visit www.drjimcostello.com or scan the QR code

•••

Printed in Dunstable, United Kingdom